BEYOND AFFAIRS

**Peggy Vaughan and
James Vaughan, Ph.D.**

DIALOG PRESS
San Diego, CA

Copyright © 1980, 1999, 2010
Peggy Vaughan and James Vaughan, Ph.D.

All rights reserved. No part of this publication may be reproduced, in whole or in part, in any form.

ISBN 978-0-936390-18-5
Manufactured in the United States of America

For information about Peggy's work,
visit her website: www.dearpeggy.com

To Vicki and Andy,
our favorite kids
and our friends

About the Authors
(Updated 2010)

Peggy Vaughan and James Vaughan, Ph.D., were the first couple to 'go public' with their own personal experience in dealing with affairs and rebuilding their marriage. This was in 1980, when this book was initially published.

During the 30 years since that time they have written 8 other books, including Peggy's classic *The Monogamy Myth*. They have dedicated themselves to helping other couples (and therapists) more effectively deal with this issue.

As of the publication of this edition of the book in 2010, Peggy and James have been married for 55 years. They were childhood sweethearts, growing up together in Mississippi. They currently live in San Diego, near their two adult children and three grandchildren.

Contents

Foreword ix

Authors' Note xi

1. What She Doesn't Know Can't Hurt Her 1
2. Young and Innocent 19
3. "When a Man Gets Excited Over a Woman, His Brain Moves Down Below His Waist" 45
4. First, The Game 69
5. It's OK to Have An Affair If... 95
6. A Time of Transition 113
7. Facing The Truth 133
8. Open Marriage? 163
9. Please Trust Me 187
10. You're Not Alone 211

Epilogue: Update 30 Years Later 227

Foreword

The discovery that a mate has had an affair is usually followed by self-searching questions in an attempt to find the cause and remedy. By opening their lives with such honesty, the Vaughans provide both men and women with new insights into the meaning of a relationship.

This is a powerful story because it's true. It's for anyone who has had an affair, or thought about it, or is in a relationship with someone who has. As a family therapist, I will recommend this book often to both individuals and couples.

> William V. Pietsch
> Author of Human BE-ing:
> *How to Have a Creative Relationship*
> *Instead of a Power Struggle*

Authors' Note

Affairs are usually conducted in secrecy and dealt with privately, if at all. Many people carry personal scars the rest of their lives, no matter which role they play—the person engaging in an affair, the partner who is left out, or the third party in the triangle. We've gained some understanding of our experience and of affairs in general by talking honestly with others involved in the same effort.

We wrote this book because we believe there's strength and support in knowing you're not alone. What happened to us has happened to many other couples—and could happen to anyone. In telling our story, we've tried to be as accurate as possible. Only the names and circumstances of others have been changed to protect their privacy.

James and Peggy Vaughan
April, 1980

About this 2010 Revised Edition

The first 10 chapters of this revised edition are the same as the original book published 30 years ago. But since many people have asked about what has happened in our marriage since that time, we decided to add an Epilogue to provide an update.

James and Peggy Vaughan
April, 2010

1

What She Doesn't Know Can't Hurt Her

James:

The first time I had lunch in New York City with Peter, his lover, and a friend from Pittsburgh, I thought, "My god, this guy is crazy. He's having an affair and he doesn't care who knows." After greeting Jane with a kiss in the lobby of his office building, he introduced her as a friend. Everyone acted as if nothing unusual were happening, so I tried to act that way too. Inside, I was anything but calm. My thoughts were racing. "Holy shit! This is really happening. How do I deal with it?"

As it turned out, there was nothing for me to deal with. I thought they might feel a need to explain their situation to me and I might have to respond in some way. Far from it. They continued to act as if everything were perfectly normal. They obviously enjoyed each other's company and didn't seem to mind including me and my friend. As it became clear they were really at ease, I relaxed too. It turned out to be an enjoyable lunch.

I had known Peter casually for about four years, but this was a complete surprise. During the following year I had lunch with him and Jane six or eight times. For them it was practically a daily ritual. I continued to be flabbergasted at their blatant openness. I thought affairs were secretive, nighttime activities. Here they were—meeting, holding hands, and kissing in broad daylight. It was either the height of craziness or real class. At the time, I concluded it was class. Now, I think it was some of both.

After I got to know Peter better, I asked him some questions about his affair.

"I don't see how you can be so close to another woman and still live with your wife. Aren't you afraid you'll slip some night at home and call your wife by your lover's name?"

"Of course not. It just doesn't happen. I've had this relationship for five years. It's easy to keep them separate."

"What if your wife surprises you by showing up at your office for lunch some day just as you're meeting Jane?"

"We live in Connecticut and my wife hates to come into the city. Besides, she doesn't go in for surprises."

"Aren't you concerned about what the people in your office think about it?"

"No, why should I be? Most of them have something of their own going."

He seemed to have it all sorted out. His answers didn't satisfy me. They were too simple and pat. I didn't have the guts to ask him the question that puzzled me most: "How can you have an affair if you still love your wife?" That one kept echoing in the back of my head.

I didn't have to ask about his love for Jane. That was clear for anyone to see. Their eye contact, their touch, and their way of talking to each other conveyed lots of love. It was fun to be with them. I didn't know exactly why at the time, but I did know it was different. Despite the length of their relationship, there was still a sense of excitement and adventure between them. Each was getting a lot of what they wanted and needed out of the relationship without the nitty-gritty responsibilities that go with a marriage or other long-term commitment.

Peter, in his mid-forties, was well-situated financially and career-wise. Jane was about my age (twenty-nine), very attractive and personable. She worked and lived alone. Sometimes they would take a long lunch hour at her apartment. Sometimes they would spend the evening together when Peter supposedly worked late. Occasionally he would stay overnight with her in the company's Manhattan apartment when it wasn't being used by other company brass, and occasionally Jane would accompany him on a business trip. They seemed to do what suited them without placing a lot of demands on each other.

During the following months, I had many reactions to Peter and Jane. At first I was shocked and non-plussed. Then I was curious. The question kept gnawing at me—"How can he keep all that in place without messing up?" I suppose my most persistent reaction was fascination. It didn't fit with the way I thought you were supposed to live, but it looked exciting. It was too far out for me to picture myself doing it at that time. I think the best evidence of this is that I'd tell Peggy after each trip all about my visit with them—including how incredulous it seemed to me. She was amazed too. Something in both of us said it was wrong, but we were too intrigued to ignore or condemn them outright.

Peggy:

The things James told me about Peter and Jane were hard to imagine. James seemed to be moving in another world—one I couldn't fully understand. It scared me that he was changing so much. I felt a little better because he told me a lot about his trips. But his traveling was hard to take. Our kids were young—just three and one. Vicki was born in 1962, about the time James started traveling. By the time

BEYOND AFFAIRS

Andy came along in 1964, he was traveling quite a bit. I was home alone with the kids while he was traveling all over the world...and I missed him terribly. We hadn't been apart a single night during the first seven years of our marriage.

In May of 1966, James asked me to go to Europe with him on a business trip. I wanted to go, but I was concerned about leaving the kids. Also, we really couldn't afford it. On the other hand, we didn't know when we'd get another chance like this. James' sister agreed to keep the kids for us—so I went.

There was a good bit of flirting going on at the conference, but I hardly noticed it. I was too excited over the trip. Also, I was terribly naive. I thought it had nothing to do with me. I trusted James completely, thinking he believed as I did—that marriage had to be monogamous. In retrospect, I can see his attitudes were changing and there was a growing likelihood of his having an affair.

James:
I was surprised when Peggy didn't pay more attention to the flirting we saw at the conference. Two respected men in my field whose wives were back in the states were openly competing for the same woman. I had known both men for about four years and assumed they were happily married. I began to get the picture that having affairs was a lot more common than I'd suspected—and it certainly wasn't limited to a few immoral scoundrels. These were men of substance and character. I probably held them in as high esteem as anyone in my professional world. Because of my positive view of them, I found it difficult to see what they were doing as bad. I saw it as amusing instead.

Without consciously realizing it, I started to think in a way that makes it easy to justify having affairs. It's really quite simple. All you have to do is hold two contradictory ideas in your mind at the same time and deny that there's any possibility of your spouse finding out. Here's what it sounds like: "It's OK for a basically honest man to be dishonest with his wife as long as he doesn't get caught. After all, what she doesn't know can't hurt her."

This thinking set the stage for my entry into the world of affairs. I hesitate to use the phrase, "world of affairs." It seems too removed and unreal. The more I think about it, the more I see it as fitting. Most people who have affairs work hard to keep them separate and removed from the mainstream of their lives. In a sense they try to create two separate lives or worlds for themselves. Some, like Peter, are very smooth at moving back and forth between their two worlds. Most of us find it too complicated and eventually something has to give. At any rate, most people who've had an affair are familiar with that world.

I took my first step into it in September, 1966. I hadn't made a conscious decision to have an affair. In retrospect, I can see that the possibility had been building in me over the past three years. The travel, the direct exposure to others having affairs, and my indifference to Peggy brought about by my career involvement—all contributed something to my readiness. The annual convention of a professional association I belonged to combined all three of these elements. Like most conventions, they provided a fertile ground for getting into affairs. They were large gatherings (upwards of 5,000) and mostly male. They were always held in large convention cities, so there was plenty of opportunity for drinking and carousing. "Ya ha time!" There was a serious working side to the convention, but for many the prime purpose was to let down their hair and have some fun.

I began attending these in 1962 as a brand new assistant professor. I went to the daytime meetings religiously. It helped me justify in my own mind the way I joined in the pursuit of fun at night. I learned to drink with the best. I watched, wide-eyed, as some of the biggest names in my field pursued the few available women with a vengeance. At that time in my life it was the most natural thing in the world to join my colleagues in this annual ritual. It seemed like everyone was doing it.

BEYOND AFFAIRS

The 1966 meeting in New York City was my fifth pilgrimage. I had learned to feel at ease with the night activities. I had not tried to pick up a woman, but I enjoyed watching others do it. I bar-hopped and went to strip shows as if I were a serious chaser. A Saturday night dance was another part of this annual ritual I managed to feel OK about dancing with women there because it was a regular convention function. I could even tell Peggy about that with a clear conscience. This year's dance was typical—lots of guys and a few women. There was one major difference for me. I was ready. I didn't know it, but I was.

I began the evening as usual, having a drink and sizing up all the goings-on from the sidelines. I didn't have it in me to make any bold moves. As the evening wore on, it looked like all those that had gone before. People were pairing up and the crowd was dwindling. I was still watching. I found myself wishing I could pick up a woman—not having a clear idea what I would do with her. "Help" came in an unusual form. About 11:30 a friend stopped by on his way out and introduced the woman he had just picked up. She suggested I look up her friend, Lisa, who had come to the dance with her. Her quick appraisal of me was that Lisa and I would enjoy each other's company. That was all the encouragement I needed. She described Lisa as a good-looking blonde in a flowing red dress. I knew from the description I hadn't seen her earlier. I was instantly excited at such a definite possibility of picking up a woman.

I began making my way around the ballroom. About ten minutes later I spotted her talking to three guys. My pulse rate jumped about thirty counts. She was good-looking, but that wasn't the main cause of my excitement. I was about to take my first step into uncharted waters. I was thirty years old. Having married at nineteen after going steady for two years, I'd had no experience in picking up women. A part of me knew this was wrong, but another part wanted to do it. I moved toward her, not knowing what I would say or do. I must have retrieved this line out of an old movie. "Lisa, I've been looking all over for you."

She took one look at me, put her hand on my arm, and said, "I'm glad you found me. I need a fresh drink."

When we had walked out of earshot of her three acquaintances, Lisa explained she was in need of being rescued. My heart was pounding like crazy. It took effort to keep my voice from shaking. I'm not even sure I succeeded. I told her about our friends hooking up and leaving me with her description. She seemed as pleased as I was that I had found her. To my surprise, she had not paired up with anyone. We danced one time and somehow I mustered the courage to take the next step.

"Why don't we stop by my hotel room for a nightcap?" It actually came out of my mouth. "Sure."

Time seemed to be speeded up. It was too simple. I don't know what I expected, but I wasn't ready for such a straightforward reply. I felt eerie and unreal as we walked out of the dance. I remember a vague concern that some of my friends might see me. At the same time, I hoped they would. Lisa was a very attractive catch.

Within thirty minutes we had walked the short distance to my hotel, found out a little about each other—including the fact that I was married and she was not—and had intercourse for the first time. It all happened so fast I could hardly believe it. I had never had intercourse with anyone but Peggy. I hadn't even kissed another woman romantically since I was seventeen. Excitement engulfed me. The normal anxiety I might have felt about doing something wrong and getting caught was submerged in the pleasure of the moment. I hadn't even had the presence of mind to ask Lisa if she had any protection. Luckily, she was on the pill.

After that first frantic screw, we relaxed and continued to get to know one another. Lisa was from the west coast. She was on her way to graduate school at a university near New York City. She was single and not involved in any kind of love relationship. In fact, she didn't even have any acquaintances at the new school she was about to enter. On my part, I told her I was happily married with two kids, that I taught organizational psychology at a university in Pittsburgh, had never before been with another woman outside my marriage, and felt very good about being with her. It was the truth. I was amazed at how good I felt. I hadn't been so excited since the first time I had intercourse with Peggy. And to my surprise, I didn't feel guilty. I had been concerned that I would. I now think it's likely that I did, but the positive feelings of excitement and pleasure just overwhelmed the guilt. I think Lisa's reaction was important. She was clearly relaxed and enjoying herself. If she had felt any guilt or regret, I think it would surely have triggered some of the same in me.

We spent the next three days together. In terms of sheer pleasure and excitement it was one of the best times I ever had. We didn't leave the hotel room until late on the second day. We ordered some food from room service and ate in the nude. We were thoroughly enjoying each other and it was pure luxury to be able to completely commit ourselves to it. We lost track of time as we talked, made love, napped, made love, and talked some more. It turned out we had lots of interests in common so we went easily from one topic to another.

Lisa had a very attractive figure and was comfortable with nudity, so I practically stayed turned on to her. She brought something else to our sex that I really liked—a playful attitude. I became aware for the first time how serious Peggy and I had become in our lovemaking. I'd always been quite satisfied with our sex life. I still was. But having something to compare it to, I could now see we were approaching it with a seriousness that was inhibiting to both of us. I think it was a reflection of our general attitude toward life. Having married at nineteen, we felt a strong need to show the world we were mature enough to handle it. Having kids intensified this feeling and added some real responsibilities to our relationship. Nobody ever called us irresponsible, but I think we overdid it. Along the way, we gave up too much of our capacity to play. I now know that wasn't necessary—especially in bed.

Lisa and I talked in depth about our pasts and things that were important to us at the time. She understood and accepted my commitment to Peggy and the kids. She was serious about getting a graduate degree and wasn't looking for a long-term relationship. I'd never disclosed so much of myself to another person in such a short time. Nor had I ever received that much from another person. I believe this part of my relationship with Lisa was just as significant for me as the sex. I know this sounds like one more rationalization for sex, but hear me out. Sex was the reason for starting the relationship. There's no doubt about that. But I was getting a bonus. I hadn't expected the level of intimacy and trust we developed. That was heady stuff. I felt a sense of freedom and personal potency that was new to me. It gave me additional ammunition to rationalize what I was doing.

"Anything this good for me that doesn't hurt Peggy or anyone else is bound to be OK. And as long as she doesn't know, how can she be hurt?" Later I would embellish this rationalization with the idea that my affairs were even benefiting Peggy by making me a better lover and generally giving me a positive outlook on life. I didn't see all this as rationalization then. I needed to feel OK about myself, so I believed it. Over the years I colluded with other men involved in affairs so we could all see ourselves as moral, trustworthy people. Now I see it was unstraight thinking, but you couldn't have made me see it then. My excitement was too high.

One of the interests Lisa and I discovered we had in common was tennis. On our third day together we went out to Forest Hills to watch some of the U.S. National Championships. I was concerned about running into someone I knew. I didn't know how I would handle it. I still felt funny being with someone else in that way, and I thought the chances of someone I knew seeing me were pretty high. This concern was the only indication of a feeling of guilt or wrongdoing I can remember. It was clear enough to get my attention but not strong enough to cause me to change what I was doing.

As we approached the entrance gate at Forest Hills we ran into Dan, a tennis-playing friend of mine from college days. I introduced Lisa as a friend. We chatted a few minutes, and he acted as if it were perfectly normal to see me with a beautiful blonde on my arm. This reassured me somewhat, but still the questions formed in my head. "What would he tell? Who would he tell? What were the possibilities of he and Peggy being together? Would it be better for me to contact him later and ask him point-blank not to mention seeing me to anyone?" I was calm on the outside, but my heart was racing.

I told Lisa about my anxieties. We couldn't help but laugh at the irony. Dan still lived in Jackson, Mississippi, where Peggy and I had developed our friendship with him. Jackson seemed a million miles away from New York City. I had not seen him in several years, but we still kept in touch. In talking through my concerns I concluded he was a pretty sophisticated guy and in all likelihood would not mention seeing us to anyone. My estimation was accurate. Peggy and I have been with him a number of times since then, and he's never even mentioned seeing me. I would learn later that most men can be trusted in this way, whether or not they have ever had an affair.

Lisa understood my concerns. She listened to them and never once showed any discomfort that I was having them. She never suggested that they were silly or that I should just forget them. She accepted me as I was—including my fears at the moment. She didn't try to change me or take care of me. She took things in stride. This was to be a very attractive characteristic she brought to our relationship.

I think this ability to accept was due to two factors. First, it was one of her basic personality strengths. She accepted herself and others in a similar way. She had obviously learned it long ago. It wasn't something she had to put effort into. Second, it was probably easier for her to accept whatever foibles she saw in me, knowing our relationship was only temporary, with a limited commitment. In marriage or any primary relationship, it's another story. Once we make a permanent commitment to another person, most of us immediately begin to form a "change" program to shape our partner into the beautiful person we want to live with. Our parents did it to us, so we know what the process is about. It's easy to justify because "it's for their own good."

The other temptation most of us succumb to in our permanent commitments is to try to take care of the feelings and emotions of our love partners—especially the upsetting ones. I don't think I know a single person who hasn't fallen into one or both of these traps in their primary relationship. I don't think it's inevitable or something that can't be changed. It's a result of the strong conditioning we receive as children to judge and evaluate—both ourselves and others—instead of to accept. It's so deeply ingrained that most of us simply accept it as the way things are. We don't realize we could learn to live differently.

Another factor which helped me keep my concerns at a low level was my general feeling of euphoria. Lisa and I were basking in the warm feelings of our new relationship. It was a beautiful, blue-sky day and life just looked too good to allow anything to interfere for long with our enjoyment. We drank in the sunshine and each other. There was excitement in our casual touch. The world looked and felt different. Lunch at a little sidewalk cafe was delicious—and the food was unimportant. Conversation came easily, but silences were also comfortable. It wasn't important to do anything. Just being together was enough. Strange as it may sound, a part of me was also pleased that we had bumped into Dan. I was scared of Peggy finding out, but I was proud that my friend had seen me with such a beautiful woman.

Lisa and I parted that first time with lots of mixed feelings. She seemed to feel as positive about our relationship as I did. So we both tried to be realistic about the future. The only trouble was, I didn't have a clear idea of what was realistic. I knew I wanted to see Lisa again. I knew I still loved Peggy as much as ever—maybe more. I also knew Lisa would be sought after by a lot of guys at school. I was afraid she would forget me in about a week. I didn't want that. I also thought it would be dumb for either of us to invest too much in the other. It just wasn't in our best self-interest. We talked about it and agreed to see each other again, but to control our emotional commitment and involvement. For two supposedly smart people, this was not so smart. It was a contradiction in terms. The control we were committing to in words just didn't fit with the excitement we were feeling inside.

On the plane back to Pittsburgh I had a weird kind of reverie. My mind seemed to race from one thought to another. Much of the time I felt like I was floating—like I could fly without the plane. I was still basking in that general euphoria. Then I would switch to concerns about Peggy finding out. I would go over details of the trip, trying to decide just how much to tell her so as to avoid any suspicion. I decided to tell her about bumping into Dan at the tennis matches. She could probably accept that; but if she found out later that we had met there and I hadn't told her, that would arouse her suspicion. Without being conscious of it, I started a strategy I would use consistently to keep Peggy from finding out—tell her as much detail as possible about my trips without giving her any information that would indict me.

Peggy generally accepted what I told her and didn't pry for other information. She knew I shared more with her than some of our friends who also traveled, so that lent some added credibility to my accounts of my whereabouts. I also decided not to lie in what I did tell her. It just didn't make sense to deliberately fabricate stories to mislead her. In the first place, I didn't think I could be a convincing liar. Secondly, the prospect of getting caught in a fabrication seemed an unnecessary complication in a lifestyle that was already complex enough.

The other awareness I remember feeling on the plane was, "Who can I tell?" I felt super. I wanted to tell the world. I felt a new enthusiasm for life. I was bursting with energy. And I know it sounds crazy, but I was bursting with love for Peggy. All in all, it was a most significant, surprising experience. The positive feelings were so strong, I completely ignored the possible negative consequences. It would be a long time before I would have the courage to face up to those.

Peggy:
I was eager for James to get back to show him the "new me." I had been dieting and changing my hairstyle while he was away. I didn't detect anything different when he first got home. He seemed to be as happy to see me as I was to see him. But a few days later there was a drastic change. He shut himself off from me emotionally and put a barrier between us.

One night soon after he got home we went to another couple's house for dinner. The other man worked with James and the four of us had been friends for quite awhile. On the way over to their house I snuggled up close to James as he drove. "You really did miss me, didn't you," he kidded.

I gave his leg an extra squeeze and cuddled even closer. I was thinking how absence really does make the heart grow fender.

When we arrived at our friends' house, James kissed the other woman hello. I felt a rush of anxiety. I didn't know what was wrong, but it was like a warning light going off in my head. We'd been married for eleven years and this was the first time he'd kissed another woman like that.

James:
My kissing Janet that night had no special significance in relation to her. I simply had a new, expansive outlook

toward the world. I felt more warmth toward everyone...and I started expressing my feelings more directly—especially with female friends.

Peggy:
As soon as we left their house, I questioned James about this change in his behavior.

"Why did you kiss Janet tonight?"

"What do you mean?"

I repeated, "Why did you kiss her? You've never done that before."

"What's the matter with you? I don't have to have a reason to kiss her."

"But there must be a reason. You don't just start doing something like that out of the clear blue sky."

"Don't be ridiculous."

I didn't expect him to be so angry. He became cold and silent. The more distant he became, the more frightened I felt. By the time we got home, his kissing Janet was the least of my worries. What scared me was the feeling of rejection I was getting from him. I kept trying to get through to him after we got home.

"What's the matter? Why are you shutting me out?" He just turned away and refused to talk. I began to feel desperate.

"Please don't turn away from me. I need you." "It's late and I'm tired."

Something seemed to be terribly wrong. I couldn't understand the isolation I was feeling.

James:
In essence I was withdrawing from Peggy—putting distance between us by setting new boundaries around what I was willing to discuss with her. I wanted to avoid getting into any discussions which might even remotely relate to my affair with Lisa.

Peggy:

I thought if James wouldn't talk to me, maybe I could get close to him through sex. But when I tried to initiate some lovemaking, he said, "No you've been too dry the last couple of days and it's caused me some soreness."

James:

That was only partly true. More to the point, I was sore from my marathon lovemaking with Lisa. I seemed to be having some kind of reaction to her chemistry. The entire end of my penis was raw.

Peggy:

I'd never felt such total rejection. I started crying, but he just lay there with his back turned. He went to sleep and left me alone with my fears. As I lay there, my fear turned to panic. I felt alone and helpless. All this seemed like a nightmare. I'd made James my whole life, and now he seemed to be rejecting me—and I didn't even know why.

I'd cried so much my head was bursting. I went to the bathroom to get some aspirin—and wished desperately that I had some sleeping pills. I wanted to die. I made it through the night, but I was shaken by the intensity of my emotions. It shocked me to realize I hadn't even considered my children or what might happen to them. In the light of day I tried to make sense of my feelings. I could see that my desperation was caused by James' rejection of me when I tried to talk to him—not by the specific incident of his kissing Janet. That was just a symptom of the real problem.

James:

I wanted to keep my relationship with Lisa neatly separate from the rest of my life. I was determined not to let if affect my marriage. I was unrealistic. The very fact that I was intent on keeping it hidden from Peggy meant that some areas of conversation were more risky now. I didn't appreciate the impact this would have on her.

BEYOND AFFAIRS

Peggy:

I could sense the invisible boundary he had set up to keep me at a distance—and I could only guess as to why. I didn't "know" he was having an affair, but I had a kind of "sinking feeling" that something bad was happening—and in a sense "knew" what it was without knowing for sure.

In later years when James was recalling the events of his first affair he placed the time as September, 1965. I said, "Are you sure?"

"Well, I think so. I know it was at a convention in New York."

"I think it had to be the meeting in September of 1966. That's when I sensed you moving away from me. I didn't know exactly what was happening at the time—but I knew it was critical."

"I guess that's right. Come to think of it, it would have been the 1966 convention."

The importance of this is not that I knew the date when James didn't, but that my sensing was so strong. I believe there are several ways to "know" something. Having facts and information is one way, and this emotional sensing is another. The intuitive feeling that your partner is having an affair can cause a great deal of pain. I believe many women "know" about affairs in this way and secretly suffer from the dilemma of what to do about it.

A lot of attention has been focused on the pain of discovering an affair, but very little on the pain of suspecting it. Only about twenty percent of the women whose husbands are having affairs ever find out for sure. That leaves eighty percent of us who supposedly don't know and therefore "can't be hurt." But we do hurt. It becomes a silent, creeping cancer that affects everything we do. It's always there—the fear, the anxiety, the uncertainty, and the enormous drain on our pride.

This pain is certainly not restricted to women, nor even to married couples. I am writing from the perspective of a married woman whose husband had affairs, because that's what I experienced. But the feelings I describe could apply to a man who suspects his wife of having an affair—or to either member of a couple who have a long-term commitment. The same is true for James' description of his experiences. It could apply to any person who is secretly having an affair. The thoughts and feelings we express are our own, but they represent an area of personal concern to almost anyone involved in a loving relationship.

2

Young and Innocent

James:
    Peggy and I have known each other all our lives. We grew up together in the same small town in Mississippi. This chapter on our early years should provide some perspective on our later experiences. It also helps to explain why Peggy was able to sense the change in me when I began having affairs. Any two people who develop the intimacy we did over a comparable period of time acquire the capacity to sense important changes in each other.
    Our early ideas about marriage were very traditional. It's likely that we were scripted for our later marriage at a tender age. When we were five years old, we lived across the street from each other. At six, we were in a "Tom Thumb" wedding. Peggy was the bride. I was the groom. My best friend married us in a make-believe church we had fashioned in the woods across the street from my house.

BEYOND AFFAIRS

That was all fun. What I didn't count on was the kidding I got from the grownups every time I went to town. I took the kidding for about two weeks, then sent Peggy a note telling her we were divorced. Looking back, I think that wedding had a lot of impact on us.

We were sweethearts off and on throughout grade school and junior high. It wasn't a constant thing, but somehow we kept coming back together. There were lots of love letters and valentines from grades one through eight, and occasionally some sweaty hand-holding in a movie or at a party. In the ninth grade we began to play for higher stakes. We started having real dates. Peggy had the cutest ass in our high school. It was just about all I could think about. Those were the days of sweaters and tight-fitting skirts. I can still remember the sight of Peggy sharpening a pencil in the front of the classroom. She had a nice motion.

I was pretty single-minded by this time. I liked Peggy and wanted to spend a lot of time with her. I didn't know enough to be thinking about intercourse yet, but when we were together, I wanted to be kissing and holding her. The feeling wasn't mutual. Peggy wanted to date me, but she wanted to keep it light. After a short time I became frustrated and stopped asking her for dates. I thought she was acting silly. I proceeded to tell everyone around our small school how childish and immature she was.

Peggy:
I was furious, but didn't say anything to James. Instead, I developed a plan to get even with him. I decided to woo him back, get him crazy about me—then drop him. I succeeded in getting him back. I soon had him head-over-heels in love with me. But then my plan fell apart. I hadn't counted on falling so much in love myself that I'd be unwilling to let him go. We were in the tenth grade by this time and old enough to start getting pretty serious.

Young and Innocent

James:

Soon after our sixteenth birthdays we were going steady and talking about our eventual marriage. We couldn't get enough of each other. We spent most of our free time together, clutching and holding one another like there was no tomorrow. At parties we danced only with each other and usually left early to spend more time alone. Both sets of parents were worried about us. They tried to discourage our getting so involved by urging us to date other people. "Play the field," begged my mother. "You're too young to tie yourself down to one person." All to no avail, their urgings may have drawn us closer together.

One vivid memory I have of this period relates to a time when Peggy was in bed for almost a week with the flu or a sore throat. The precise reason for her being in bed was not so important. The significant thing was the new experience it provided. All I can remember is how her breasts felt under those maroon silk pajamas—with no bra. It was almost more than my young heart could take. I was supposed to go directly to basketball practice after school, but I would sandwich in about thirty minutes of feeling-up time first. That was one of the most enjoyable times of my life. Pure excitement! I can still feel it right now. It's delicious. Everyone ought to experience it at least once. It would be great to experience it again and again, but that kind of innocence only occurs once in a lifetime.

Peggy:

For the next few months we were totally engrossed in each other. It was a time of gradually increasing the amount of petting we did—but always with a feeling of conflict over whether or not it was OK. My Southern Baptist upbringing had given me a strong dose of guilt about such things. I was very active in church activities, and that summer after the tenth grade I spent a couple of weeks in another town working with a youth crusade. I also sang in the choir and sang solos in church, as well as at weddings and funerals.

BEYOND AFFAIRS

It was this participation in church music that led to a major crisis. Our church had a mid-summer revival, and a visiting preacher came to conduct the services. Also, a young ministerial student came to conduct the music for the revival. Chris was a bachelor and a lot of girls in the choir flirted with him. I did not. Nevertheless, he singled me out as the one he wanted to get to know. James was out of town and I had no inclination to get involved with anyone else. I felt no fear, however, in talking to him. After all—he was a minister. Little did I suspect he was out to convince me I had been "chosen" to be his wife and to work with him in the service of the church. He was very persuasive. But more importantly, this fit with the secret fears I'd always had about something bad happening to me if I didn't commit my life to some religious work.

I felt terrible to be breaking up with James, but I didn't think I had a choice. I knew I could never make James understand, so I decided to say as little as possible.

James:
This happened in late July while I was in Washington, D.C. for a two-week visit with my older sister. I missed Peggy something fierce and could hardly wait to get back home. I wasn't prepared for the shock of what had happened while I was away. I don't think it could have happened if I'd been there. But with me gone and Peggy still feeling that internal religious conflict, he hit a responsive chord. To be "called to God's service" was more than she could withstand.

I could hardly believe it. In fact, I refused to believe it. I felt sure I could straighten everything out if we could just talk about it. We loved each other too much to call it off that abruptly. I also smelled a big rat in the deal. It's one thing to be called to God's service. It's something else to be called to be some joker's wife.

But Peggy wouldn't talk about it. She gave me the bare facts and then refused to discuss it further. In fact, she refused to see me anymore—period. For the first and only time in my life, I was really depressed. I didn't want to accept it. I moped. I got a lot of encouragement from family and friends to date other girls, but I wasn't interested. I wanted Peggy. And I thought she still loved me. I was pretty sure her refusal to see me at all was her way of coping with that. I knew she was serious about her religious beliefs. I just couldn't buy the idea that I had to be ruled out of her life.

Peggy:

I made a lot of changes in my life. I had been a majorette, but when school started I didn't rejoin the band. I stopped going to movies. I stopped going to dances. I felt I had to stop being frivolous and get serious about my religious role. There's a lot more to my feelings about religion than I can go into in this book. Someday I may write about my early experiences in the church and the changes in my perspective through the years. For now I'll stick to the parts that directly affected my relationship with James.

I feel sure if I had been old enough, I would have gone ahead and married Chris then. But I still had two more years of high school. At school I couldn't avoid seeing James as I'd done during the summer. We shared all the same classes. It was torture to see him every day and have to stay away from him. Also, I began to face up to some things about Chris that caused me to rethink my decision. He wanted to do the same kinds of petting James had wanted to do. I couldn't see any difference between them except that he would have us get on our knees and pray about the strength of our physical desires. I think he was sincere about his commitment to the church, and I think he was sincere about wanting me to join him in that commitment. But it didn't come with all the idealistic purity I had envisioned.

I still loved James, and I was torn as to what to do. I finally decided I wanted to go back to James, but I thought it might be too late. I wouldn't have blamed him if he hadn't taken me back. I couldn't bring myself to ask him directly. I didn't think I deserved him now after hurting him. I finally confided my feelings to Carol, my best friend.

James:
After about three months of complete separation, I was surprised when Carol told me Peggy wanted to date me again. I didn't have to be told twice. I remember one of my sisters being disgusted with me. She said I shouldn't take her back—that I had no pride. To hell with pride. I knew what I wanted. I loved Peggy and I wanted to live my life with her. With high excitement and considerable trepidation, we started dating again. It took some time for us to get ourselves back together. The desire was there on both our parts, but Peggy's recent experience had left its mark. There were some new reservations about the rightness of the kind of petting we had been doing before. I was patient, and slowly we worked through to what was important to both of us—that we loved each other.

Try to get a picture of where we were in our lives. We were young and innocent. We were almost seventeen years old. We were juniors in high school. We were going steady and constantly talking about our love and eventual marriage.

I had almost total use of my family's '48 Chevrolet. This was a very significant part of our lives. Living in a small town surrounded by farms and lots of open land, we were able to get complete privacy almost daily by parking in out-of-the-way places. We could never have moved so far in our petting if we had been confined to either of our homes. We had both been raised in homes with Christian values and morals. Not overly strict, but clear. The upshot was, we found ourselves in a tremendous struggle.

Our bodies said, "This feels too good to be wrong."
But our consciences said, "We shouldn't be doing this."
Over a period of several months our petting kept getting heavier and heavier. First just having Peggy's bra unsnapped was enough. Taking it off completely was even better, although it took quite awhile for her to feel comfortable with

this—even with her blouse still on. Taking that off too was another giant step. Especially in the daytime. I loved it at night, but in the daytime, the sight of her breasts heightened the feelings for me dramatically. Once I had experienced the sight and feel of her naked breasts, there was no going back.

We finally worked up to the point of having Peggy completely undressed except for keeping her slip bunched up around her waist. I suppose there was something symbolic about that. It was probably a reminder that we couldn't go all the way. We hadn't yet worked through all those contradictory messages we kept hearing in our heads. I think I was ready to go ahead before Peggy was, but I didn't want to push her into something she would regret. I wanted a long-term relationship with her and I didn't want to jeopardize it for some short term pleasure—even that short term pleasure. We had long conversations about what was right and wrong. We both started with the notion that intercourse before marriage was wrong. Now we were asking each other, "Why? Why does a marriage certificate make it OK to have intercourse? Isn't it more important to love each other? And if you love each other and are committed to each other for life, isn't that enough?" Our bodies were saying, "Yes." But our consciences kept saying, "No." The debate continued. Slowly but surely, our bodies were winning. It seemed inevitable that we would begin having intercourse before too long.

One afternoon in April we had an honest-to-goodness show and tell in Peggy's bedroom. By now, I had fondled her vagina many times, as she had my penis. But we had never allowed ourselves the luxury of really looking at each other's genitals. In fact, Peggy had never used a mirror to look at her own genitals. So we looked and satisfied our curiosities. It was a very positive experience. I think it was the last bit of adult checking out we needed to do to assure ourselves we knew what we were doing and it was OK to go ahead and express our love with intercourse. Shortly afterwards, I bought some prophylactics and we finally "did it." It was fantastic! It had taken a lot of head-work to subdue our absolute teachings against it, but we had done it.

Peggy:
Arriving at this point was a long struggle for me—especially with the overtones of sin and the guilt I felt about it. But I did love him and he loved me, and waiting any longer just didn't seem reasonable. There was no question in my mind that I would spend the rest of my life with him. But there was quite a long wait before we could officially begin that life together.

James:
This was the beginning of one of the most enjoyable periods of my life. We made love on most of the back roads of Monroe County. We had to keep moving around since most of the kids our age were also into parking, and we weren't willing for anyone to know about our level of intimacy. It wasn't much of a problem to find a private place at night. The kids who weren't going all the way preferred to congregate in a few favorite spots. We just kept up with which spots were popular and made a point to go somewhere else.

Finding a suitable place in the daytime was a challenge of a different magnitude. We had to be completely out of sight and in a place where no one was likely to happen along. At night you could at least count on the glare of headlights to provide a little forewarning of an approaching car. And even if you couldn't recover completely, it was unlikely anyone would ever stop to investigate since parked cars at night were common in the area. Not so in the daytime. If anyone did happen down the same dirt road we chose, we had little chance of detecting them until they were upon us. And because of the relative isolation of the spots, it was likely that any visitors would stop to investigate. All that awareness didn't deter us, however. It probably just increased the excitement.

Young and Innocent

Ah, those Sunday afternoon rides. The summertime was best. You haven't lived until you've cruised the back country roads on a hot summer afternoon looking for just the right spot. We would begin fooling around as soon as we were out of town. Sometimes we would be so excited by the time we found a spot, we could hardly wait to get our clothes off. Nighttime was good, but I preferred the day. I've always liked that added dimension of seeing what's happening. The perspiration on those summer days added still another dimension. Sometimes we would be so sweaty we could hardly hold onto each other.

For years I've referred to this time as our period of "young hot love." What we lacked in technique and sophistication, we made up for with desire and enthusiasm. It was a grand time. Of course, we didn't fully appreciate it then. We still found ways to feel deprived. We longed to do it in a bed. We just knew it had to be better. I think the bed represented more than sheer comfort for us. It meant sanction and freedom. We resented having to hide and live with the other physical restrictions of the car. Occasionally, we'd spread a beach towel or blanket outside the car. This provided a pleasant change, but it was no substitute for a bed.

Since we had no basis for comparison, we couldn't know just how good our situation was. The back seat of the old Chevy was actually a super place to do it. The possibilities for bracing yourself were far superior to a bed. And there was ample room. The fact we were not free to do it every day or night actually heightened the anticipation and enjoyment of the times when we could manage it. We know now that it's extremely difficult to maintain that level of excitement in ongoing sex when facing the other day-to-day issues of living together.

The other thing we grew to resent was the use of prophylactics. At first it was not an issue. Our excitement was so great we didn't notice them. It was a small nuisance compared to the amount of enjoyment we were getting.

BEYOND AFFAIRS

Gradually, this changed. As we got braver with our experimentation, I would rub my bare penis on Peggy's vagina and even insert it briefly. The feel of skin on skin was lovely. We began to long for the day when we wouldn't have to use anything between us. In addition to inhibiting physical sensation, prophylactics detracted from the beauty of the whole experience. First, we had to interrupt the flow of lovemaking at a point when the excitement was building. And even with practice, it's not easy to get the thing on without substantially altering the mood. Then there was the second interruption which we disliked even more. After climax we liked to hold one another with the penis still inserted. This is still one of the most enjoyable parts of lovemaking for us. We soon learned though, that we ran a high risk of the prophylactic slipping off, especially in the summer with the extra lubrication. But we resented having to break the mood before we were ready.

Looking back, these were minor distractions in light of the overall pleasure and nourishment we were getting from our growing relationship. In addition to being lovers, we became best friends. We spent many hours talking about all aspects of our lives and planning the life we wanted to share in the future. I suppose our fear of letting anyone else know about our sexual intimacy drew us even closer. We each had a same-sex friend we were quite close to, but we didn't tell anyone what was happening with us.

Learning about sex together was an exciting adventure. Neither of us had been told more than the basic facts by our parents. I had heard a fair amount of locker room talk, but it was worthless in terms of providing any real information about lovemaking. We learned by doing and talking about what happened. We were very innocent. This turned out to be a positive thing for us, primarily because we really cared for each other and were sensitive to each other's needs. We don't recommend that degree of innocence, however. The potential dangers are too great. For example, if I had pushed Peggy into intercourse before she was ready, she might have been left with guilt feelings that would have been very difficult to shed. Of course, the same possibility exists for the guy, but in our case, I think Peggy's risks for guilt were higher than mine. In our generation, society placed the burden on the female to resist premarital sex. Generally, males were more quickly forgiven for such transgressions since they presumably had more uncontrollable urges during this period of growth. Of course, these attitudes are slowly changing, but unfortunately, many people still think this way.

Perhaps an even greater danger was that Peggy could have gotten pregnant. Given our parents and the attitudes that prevailed in our small community, there's no way to predict how we would have come through that. It's fair to say, it would have produced some trauma. Even assuming our parents could have dealt with their own embarrassment and supported us psychologically and emotionally, starting our married life at eighteen with a child would have been very different from the way we eventually began.

Peggy:
I felt all the excitement James felt, but I also continued to be upset by the sneakiness and secretiveness of our lovemaking. My parents were concerned about what we might be doing. Breakfast was usually a time when they asked me questions about how late I was out and where we went. They never asked me point-blank what we were doing sexually, but I knew that was the reason for the questions. I felt like a criminal trying to conceal a crime. I cried a lot and longed for the time when we wouldn't have to sneak around.

We were seniors in high school and wanted desperately to get married as soon as we graduated. Both sets of parents approved of our eventual marriage, but wanted us to go to college first. We couldn't imagine waiting that long. So we came up with a compromise. James would go to college for one year while I lived at home and worked to save money, so we could get married at the end of that year.

BEYOND AFFAIRS

Everything looked good when we graduated from high school in May of 1954, but it very nearly didn't work out the way we planned. Things started OK. I began my job as a secretary the week after graduation, and James started to summer school at the University of Mississippi. Our concern about the military service intervening if he postponed college led us both to assume I'd be the one to work while he went to school. We saw education as more important for him than me. We were thoroughly conditioned in the traditional roles of men and women.

Our major concern was our frustration at being separated except when he came home on weekends. We made it through the summer, but the intensity of our lovemaking increased. We continued to use caution about birth control, but in September I missed my period. I was terrified that I might be pregnant. I'd never had regular periods and probably shouldn't have been so concerned. But I just couldn't keep from being scared.

By early October we decided to get secretly married—just in case. It turned out I wasn't pregnant. We were tremendously relieved. But we decided not to tell anybody about our marriage. We thought it best to go through with our plans for being formally married at the end of the school year.

In the meantime, we made some drastic changes in our sex life. We had been terribly shaken by thinking I might be pregnant, so we vowed not to take any more chances. We decided to stop having intercourse until our formal wedding. We tried to find other ways of satisfying each other sexually. Since we were legally married, I no longer felt guilty about sex and felt free to do things I would have felt bad about doing before. We didn't, however, engage in oral sex. We didn't even know there was such a thing. In fact, we didn't learn about oral sex and include it as part of our sex life until we were thirty-four years old.

There were other major changes that year. In January, James transferred from "Ole Miss" to Millsaps College in

Young and Innocent

Jackson, Mississippi, as a preministerial student. I was pleased at his decision, but I hadn't suggested it. He was doing it out of his own conviction. Since James was Methodist, I joined the Methodist Church three weeks before we got married.

We had a beautiful wedding on May 29, 1955, with all our friends and family—just as planned. We drove to Jackson that same day and checked into a motel. We were ecstatic to finally have a bed to make love in. I was fitted for a diaphragm soon after we married, and that was another wonderful change. Now we could have intercourse again after all those months of waiting and we could have it without the barrier and interruptions of using prophylactics.

James:

In some ways we had built a very strong relationship. Having been lovers and best friends for so long, we entered marriage with a high level of openness. We kept no secrets from each other and there were no major unknowns in either of our pasts. We didn't realize the importance of our openness at the time. Over all, we were very naive about the realities of maintaining a good relationship. Physical attraction had been an important part of our coming together and was still important to us. That's not bad, but it's also not enough. The most dangerous part of our innocence had to do with our beliefs about romantic love. We truly believed we had a special love. And we bought two key all-American myths: "Love conquers all," and "A marriage based on true love leads to blissful fulfillment forever." Love helps in the face of many difficult situations, but so do a lot of other things like patience, understanding, and the willingness to work through the myriad of differences in needs, preferences, and values that are bound to arise between two people.

"The two shall become one." Our early interpretation of this was that we should do the same things, like the same things, and generally stick together. We were active churchgoers during this period, and we got strong reinforcement there for these notions. "The family that prays together stays together." As well as "The family that plays together stays together." One result was I felt guilty to play tennis on a Sunday afternoon when Peggy chose not to, and she usually denied herself any activities that didn't include me. Probably the only thing that kept us from smothering each other was the fact that both our lives were pretty heavily structured with a combination of college classes and outside work. I was going to school full time and working part time. Peggy was working full time and going to school part time. The negative side of our heavy schedules was that new stresses and strains were introduced into our relationship, and we hadn't left much time just for us. Going into marriage with a strong bond helped us survive those early years, but I now see we weren't actively building and maintaining our relationship in a way I think is possible.

Peggy:
We were romantic and idealistic in some ways, but we were also intent on showing the world we were mature enough to handle marriage. In fact, I think I tried to be a little too mature about the whole thing. The joy of being together was dampened by the serious way I approached my role as a wife. I was dedicated to working very hard and doing everything that could possibly be expected of me. I had a full-time job, took three courses at school, and still tried to be the perfect housewife. I cooked biscuits every morning. I made homemade rolls each week. I ironed a white shirt for James to wear every day to his part-time job downtown. In short, I submerged myself in my new role.

One of the drawbacks to this was that I depended on James to meet all my needs for approval. As a teenager I had gotten a lot of approval in the form of being "popular" and being considered pretty and talented. After we got married I stopped looking for approval from others and relied solely on James. My image of myself was totally tied into doing a good job as his wife. At the time I thought I was doing exactly the right thing. It's only from my present perspective that I can see how damaging that was to my confidence and self-esteem. I set myself up as a second-class citizen, devoted to James' comfort and service. It was easy for him to begin seeing me as my role instead of the person he married.

James:
   Sure enough, I changed my way of thinking about Peggy during these first three years of marriage. It was a gradual change and I've only recently realized the significance of it. I started to view Peggy less as an individual and more as a woman (stereotypically)—one of "them." It happened like this. As I developed some closeness with other men at work and playing tennis, we talked about the surface issues we were having with our wives. Actually, it was moralizing. The punch line always had an "ain't it awful" flavor to it.
   "Ain't it awful that our wives don't understand our need to play tennis?"
   "Yeh, and ain't it awful that they get emotional and cry instead of rationally discussing things like we do?" "Ain't it awful that they can't deal with time pressure the way we do?"
   The conclusion: "Women are different. They are emotional. They don't deal with things the way we (men) do. That's the way they are. We'll never be able to understand them or change them, so we may as well accept them as they are. It's tough to live with them, but tougher to live without them. Slowly, but surely, I joined the mass of men who view women not as individuals, but as members of a mysterious group.
   This is a separating attitude. When faced with a difference, it allowed me to lump Peggy into a difficult group rather than deal with her directly. It was easy to find sympathy and support from other men. And still is. I find it extremely rare to be with a group of men discussing women

and not have some of these stereotypes expressed. Most men are not being consciously malicious. They really believe that's the way things are. Or they simply haven't stopped to examine their way of thinking about women.

Peggy:
Some of the stereotypical ideas are based on the fact that as a group we have tended to be emotional. But I see this as a reasonable result of the traditional role we've played in relation to men, sacrificing and subjecting ourselves to a position of less importance. Given the unreasonableness of the role I was taking on myself, it was perfectly understandable that I would be frustrated, upset, insecure—and yes, emotional. Any person, man or woman, playing that role would be likely to react the same way.

James:
I was not even aware my ways of thinking about and relating to Peggy were changing. I thought I was just doing what all married men had to do—learn to live with women. I now believe this attitude provides a fertile ground for affairs. Especially when you have them in the traditional male double standard like I did. It's easier to justify an affair when you're thinking of your wife as one of them instead of as an individual.

The possibility of extramarital affairs was not something I even thought about during those early years of marriage, much less discussed. I had grown up in a sheltered environment in that regard. Any affairs that occurred in our hometown were matters of deep shame. So far as I know, both my parents were totally committed to monogamy, but the clearest expressions of their beliefs came from Mother. To her, marriage was and is a sacred institution. The idea of extramarital sex was repulsive, and the reality was something she chose to ignore. Above all, it was not a topic to discuss with children. Whenever the topic did arise at home, she was always quick to make it clear that unfaithfulness should never occur, and if it did, it was too awful to talk about. Since I had no direct knowledge of anyone having an affair while growing up, I think Mother's views made up most of my early information and attitudes about affairs.

Peggy:
My earliest memories about extramarital affairs are pretty vague. I do remember the words used to describe someone who was having an affair. They were "stepping out" on their husband or wife. It was clear that anyone who did this was a "no-good" character. Only a low-class person would do such a thing. I certainly couldn't imagine anyone I knew being that kind of person. The whole issue was nothing I saw as relevant to my life.

This naive attitude toward the prevalence of affairs was understandable during our early years of marriage. The environment at Millsaps for the first three years was in many ways just as cloistered as our childhood had been. We lived on campus with other preministerial students. We knew no one who had affairs.

During the years that followed, however, we broadened our exposure to the world considerably. James accepted a scholarship to Yale Divinity School and attended one semester, but he'd fallen in love with psychology. We'd both become disillusioned with traditional religious teachings, and he made the difficult decision of switching from the ministry to psychology. This decision involved moving to Middletown, Connecticut, where he got a Master's degree in Clinical Psychology at Wesleyan University. From there we went to Baton Rouge, Louisiana, where he got a Ph.D. in Industrial Psychology at Louisiana State University.

During those four years of his graduate training I worked full time at various jobs: two different jobs at college libraries, a job as a legal secretary, and another as a secretary to a contractor. I was learning a lot about the ways of the outside world, and about the world of marriage in particular.

James:
We were gradually becoming aware that marriage was not the ideal state society held it up to be. We sometimes were included in speculative conversations about who was fooling around with whom. Still, it never occurred to us that either of us might ever fool around. If we had seen first-hand some of the consequences and the frequency of affairs, we probably would have taken more notice of them. During these early years of our marriage we were not touched directly by any family or close friends having affairs, so we continued to see them as something that happened occasionally to others. Our strong assumption was that couples who loved as we did were simply immune.

Peggy:
I was the first to discover we were not immune. Through my work experience I met a married man who became interested in me. Alex constantly commented on my intelligence, my ability, and my appearance. His success and sophistication were unlike anything I had known before. I was impressed that such a man found me attractive and desirable. I think the reflection of yourself you see through someone else's eyes is a powerful force in any attraction. I know this was an important part of what was happening to me. But at the time, I was thoroughly confused by the whole situation—especially my own feelings. I became fascinated with him, but I was afraid to discuss any of this with James. I was afraid even to admit it to myself.

I composed a lecture to Alex: "If you feel compelled to have an affair, I feel sure you can find plenty of willing partners, but I couldn't do such a thing." I never delivered the lecture. I was trying to be brave for both of us. It completely scrambled my thinking when I discovered he had been involved in affairs for years. It would seem this might have shocked me out of my fascination with him. Instead, it just increased it. Even as I was becoming enamored of him, I kept telling myself it couldn't be happening. Things like that just didn't happen to people like me—meaning good, moral people who are married and completely committed to their marriage.

The key scene that led to confronting these feelings occurred late one afternoon when we were the last people to leave a meeting—and found ourselves alone. We had never openly acknowledged the attraction between us. But on this occasion he changed all that. He stood across the room from me and said, "Come over here. I want you to meet someone." At that moment my head spun wildly as I hung in the balance between walking to him or staying away. I don't remember deciding, but I did walk to him—and he kissed me.

I couldn't believe my feelings. Kissing him was very much against my values. It upset me terribly—but I enjoyed it. This kissing scene was repeated often and the longer it went on the more distraught I became. I had fallen in love with him, but I felt I would destroy my marriage if I went to bed with him. I loved James and wanted to stay married. I was in limbo. I stayed upset most of the time and cried a lot. Finally, after about six months of kissing and clutching and teetering on the brink, we agreed to stop torturing ourselves and bring things to a halt before they went any further. The experience left me shaken. I saw how easy it would have been to have an affair, and it scared me terribly to have come so close.

All this had a lasting effect on me. I vowed never to allow the possibility of being attracted to anyone again. Another important effect was to destroy my illusion that marriage—any marriage—was safe from this threat. This was marked indelibly in my mind and was a major factor in the suspicions I had later when James was out in the business world and I was at home.

BEYOND AFFAIRS

James:
 I didn't learn of this experience until years later when I told Peggy about my affairs. Although I knew Alex quite well and considered him one of my best friends, I never had the slightest suspicion of his intentions or actions with Peggy. From my point of view the whole incident is important as an example of how naive and unaware I was at the time. I think anyone who is in touch with their spouse and realistic about the possibility of affairs will sense over a six month period if she is involved or about to be involved with someone else. Peggy was emotionally distraught during the whole thing. In a sense she "told" me about it with lots of tears—which I interpreted as the natural emotionality of a woman. In fact, Alex and I had many moralizing conversations about this aspect of women. One of us would usually end these conversations with something like, "Well, that's the way they are; we might as well accept it. But if we could ever figure them out, we could make a million." Believe me, it's humbling to realize that all this time he knew what Peggy's tears were about, and I was practically unconscious.

 The growing separation which I described during the first three years of our marriage had continued to the point where I was seeing Peggy more and more as one of "them" instead of my wife. By now I had been part of many conversations with fellow graduate students where we shared our miseries of married life. It was very seductive. There always seemed to be somebody complaining about their wife and somebody else responding, "Yeh, I know what you mean. It's tough."

Peggy:
 In 1962 a major transition took place in our lives. James finished school, and I quit work and had our first child. During the last few years of my working days when James was still a student, I'd begun to feel I was outgrowing him—that I was more mature and sophisticated. I didn't like that.

Young and Innocent

The expectations I grew up with said this wasn't the way marriage was supposed to be. I was anxious to get things in their "proper" place—with me a full-time mother and homemaker and James as the financially responsible head of the house.

James was due to finish all his coursework in May and begin teaching, so we decided that was the time to start our family. I was fortunate to conceive within one month of the time we began trying. It was a happy time in my life. I felt good throughout the pregnancy and worked until a couple of months before I was due. I stayed busy preparing for my new role. I was an only child, and I had never taken care of any children while growing up. I wanted to know everything. I studied constantly about childbirth and child care, and gained a lot of knowledge and confidence in my ability to deliver and care for the baby. James was excited by the prospect of being a father too. It was a time of much closeness for us as a couple.

Vicki was born on May 18, 1962. She was a darling, healthy baby. I loved being a mother. Life looked great.

James:

It looked great to me too. Up to this time my primary identity in life had been as a student. I had been in college and graduate school for eight years beyond high school. Peggy had been the mainstay in my personal support system for the entire period, both physically and psychologically. Although I received some positive strokes for my success as a student, my general sense of myself was that I was behind in life. I had some catching up to do in terms of accumulating some of the physical things that symbolized success. I had not developed a sense of who I was as a competent, independent person.

It's paradoxical. While actually being a member of a privileged minority who had the opportunity to finish a graduate degree, I was feeling like a second-class citizen. I think the competitive nature of the Ph.D. program I was in had a lot to do with this. Fear was one of the primary motivators. It was made crystal clear to us that we would not all finish the program. Some of us would win (pass all the requirements and get our Ph.D.'s) and some would lose (fail a requirement and get dropped from the program). It made it rather difficult to develop lasting relationships with fellow students. We were literally competing for the right to stay in the program in every class.

When you give others the right to accept or reject you over such a long period of time, it does something to you. It's difficult to maintain a sense of your own worth. I was constantly comparing myself with friends who had taken jobs right out of high school and who now owned homes and seemed to be established members of the community. I knew I didn't want the lifestyle they had chosen, but I couldn't stop making the comparisons and coming up short. Even when I seemed to be doing well in my degree program, there was the ever present fear that I might not pass the language exam or that a single faculty member on my final committee might dislike me and flunk me at the very end. We all had these fears to some degree. We tried to be realistic about them, but it was hard to do away with them completely. My relationship with Peggy was an important stabilizer for me during this period, which seemed like an interminable time in my life.

All this changed in the space of three months. In September, 1962, I went from a scrounging graduate student, being supported by my wife—to a faculty member at a university in Pittsburgh, supporting a wife and child in suburbia. I began to see myself as a breadwinner. I threw myself into teaching and research and left the care of Vicki primarily to Peggy. We had both wanted kids all along and this fit our image of how it should happen.

Peggy:
There were some surprises. The changes for me were much more difficult than I had expected. I hadn't counted on

the lost feeling I would have when we moved to Pittsburgh and I was deposited out in the suburbs with the baby and no car, with James gone most of the time with the demands of his new job.

Despite the drawbacks, I really loved being a mother, and I wanted to have another child when Vicki was two years old. Again we succeeded within one month of trying to conceive. Andy was born on June 27, 1964, just two years and one month after Vicki. He was a beautiful, healthy boy. Now we had a girl and a boy—the all-American family. While I took a lot of joy in the children, James was too busy with his own life directions to stay tuned in to us.

His job took most of his time and energy. But he also spent a lot of time playing tennis. I frequently felt his work came first, tennis second, and I had to wait for whatever time might be left over. I resented this and wanted him to spend more of his time with me and the kids. One of the most outrageous incidents around this issue occurred at the time of Andy's birth. James was playing in the West Penn Tennis Tournament. I was pregnant and due any day. While watching him play I had some labor pains and realized I had to go directly to the hospital. He let a friend take me while he stayed to finish his match. Fortunately, James arrived at the hospital before Andy was born.

James:

It hurts to admit how insensitive I was to Peggy during this period. I remember the disappointment I felt when I was about to walk on the court to play a semi-final match and she told me she had to go to the hospital. It must have shown in my face. A friend who was there to watch me play quickly spoke up, "I've got my car. I'll be glad to take her." "Would you?" I responded. "Gee, that would be great. Then I'll come right over after I finish my match." I wish I could blame it on the sun. Any clod ought to be more tuned in than that.

BEYOND AFFAIRS

With Andy on the scene our new lifestyle was well established. Peggy was a confirmed wife and mother. Those two roles formed her total identity. I was a professional psychologist, playing the university game to the hilt. Like most of my colleagues, I was a husband and father, but that was secondary to our work at the university. It was assumed that everyone had a family. The trick was not to let that interfere with your career.

Without being aware of it, we had now settled into the mainstream of the American way of arranging family role responsibilities that sets the stage for one or both partners to lose interest in the marriage and gain interest in someone outside the marriage. Most of the nitty-gritty, day-to-day care of small babies had little or no appeal for me, so I gladly left that to Peggy. She accepted it as her proper role.

Having been a lowly graduate student for what seemed like a lifetime, I was finding the life of a faculty member to be rather agreeable. Having my own private office, eating lunch at the faculty club, serving on Dean's Councils, being called "Dr. Vaughan"—all this was heady stuff. I hate to admit it, but it's clear I became infatuated with the importance (as I saw it) of my work at the university.

I overvalued that and undervalued the work Peggy was doing with the kids. It's not that I was completely uninvolved at home. I changed some diapers and even enjoyed some aspects of that early child care. Down deep though, I thought this was basically women's work. I had grown up with this attitude, and now it was being reinforced by my university colleagues. We all valued our families and realized someone had to take care of the homefront. But that's what wives were for. Our work was the really important stuff of life. It's hard to believe I really thought that way—but I did.

Peggy:
While James was putting all his energies into his career, I was devoting all my time to taking care of the house and

kids. We had come to a fork in the road. Without consciously choosing it, we were heading in different directions. I never dreamed how far we would go before we finally realized what was happening to us.

3

"When a Man Gets Excited Over a Woman, His Brain Moves Down Below His Waist."

Peggy:
My trust in James during the early years of our marriage had slowly disintegrated. By the time he began his first affair in 1966, the closeness I once felt had turned to isolation. During the seven years while he was involved in affairs he became something of a stranger. I never knew whether the image he presented to me was real or not. He talked about other people and their affairs in such a superior, above-it-all way that I was confused as to what he really thought. I was scared, but didn't trust my feelings. I kept thinking I might be imagining things.

One thing I wasn't imagining was the new emphasis James was putting on his looks. He went on a diet and lost a lot of weight. I was afraid he might be doing it to impress another woman.

BEYOND AFFAIRS

James:
    Lisa and I had both talked about losing some weight. Prior to meeting her I had slowly inched up to the most I had ever weighed—184 pounds. I had been thinking about going on a diet, but hadn't quite been able to muster the willpower. Now I had the motivation. I didn't feel old at thirty, but I was aware of the eight year difference in our ages. I wanted to make myself as attractive as possible. I was delighted to find I had lost four pounds during the three days I had spent with her. That, plus my general feeling of being on top of the world, gave me the start I needed. I began eating salads for lunch—sometimes just carrots and celery. It seemed effortless. I had a powerful reason to get fit and trim. The net result was I lost twenty-four pounds in six weeks. My friends who knew how I loved to eat just watched the pounds melt away in disbelief. That added to my enjoyment of the whole process. They couldn't believe it was real. I knew it was real and I also knew why.
    I saw Lisa several times during the next six months. Whenever I had a business trip to New York City, I would call a few days in advance and invite her to join me. Even when a colleague was traveling with me I always took a single room, so that part was easy. We were a little nervous at first that some hotel clerk might notice us coming in and out and question my single room status. I would check in and she would come up to the room a little later. It added a little extra excitement to our meetings. Later on we got rather blase about it and Lisa would even stop by the desk and ask for a second key. Luckily, we never had any problems in that area.
    I was surprised and pleased that Lisa seemed as eager to get together as I was. No matter what part of the week I was in town she managed to find a way to spend part of it with me. It was about a ninety-minute train ride into the city for her. Whenever we could coordinate it I would meet her at the station, but when the timing wasn't right for that, she would get herself to the hotel. If she were in a particularly

When a Man Gets Excited Over a Woman...

busy time at school, she would spend only one night—at other times two or three. I was involved in business meetings during the day, but always free at night. Sometimes she would explore the city while I was working. Other times she would study in the hotel room. We practically never did anything in the city at night. We were really into each other and spent most evenings talking and making love.

Another factor which added to our good times together was the fact that we were able to stay in pleasant places. I got a special faculty rate at a couple of the finest hotels in New York by virtue of my university job. So we always had attractive surroundings. Sometimes, they would have filled all their single rooms and I'd get a large double or even a suite for my single faculty rate. That was fun. If either of us had felt the necessity to meet in some sleazy, out-of-the-way hotel, that probably would have had a dampening effect. But the positive surroundings increased the feelings that this was a good thing to be doing and prevented my seeing some of the negatives.

Peggy:
James knew I was having a hard time dealing with his traveling so much. Shortly before Christmas he told me he had to make a trip to New York between Christmas and New Year's and wanted me to come with him. I was surprised, but happy he wanted me to go. He would be working with another man whose wife would be going also.

It had been less than four months since the convention in New York when he began his affair. He had made several trips to New York since then. I was afraid he might have been seeing someone on those trips, so I was on the lookout for things he might say or do while I was with him. Everything went well until one night James took us by a little kielbasa food stand he'd raved about. As we stood there eating, I had the distinct feeling he wouldn't have discovered kielbasa all by himself and wouldn't have found this little stand-up food store so exciting if he were alone. I felt in my gut this had to be a place he usually went with another woman.

James:
Peggy's intuition was right. It was a place Lisa and I had discovered, so it had a special significance. They served great German sausage, but not that great. Lisa and I sometimes ate good meals in fine restaurants, but more often than not we ate very simply in little out-of-the-way places. She was fascinated, as I was, with New York City, and we enjoyed finding different eating places off the beaten path. I think Lisa was also sensitive to the costs of the better restaurants, and since I paid for our meals, this was one way she could help keep my expenses in line. Eating was not that important to us anyway. We were getting our kicks out of being together.

Peggy:
I was especially busy for the first few days after we got home from New York, so I didn't spend much time dwelling on my concerns. I turned my attention to preparing for a New Year's Eve party we were to attend. I'd bought a harem dress pattern and some sparkly material to make a special party dress. I had only two days to get it done. I might not have bothered except that I saw every social occasion, especially involving the women he worked with, as a special challenge. I think I focused on the women he worked with because they were a known entity as opposed to unknown women in his travels. I figured if I could make James feel he had a terrific wife, he wouldn't be as tempted to go out with other women. I even bought a strapless push-up bra to wear to the party to try to look especially sexy. I didn't stop with working on my looks though. I felt I must compare favorably with any potential competition in any area. I worked hard at being a good dancer. I loved to dance anyway, but now I became serious about it. I didn't know

When a Man Gets Excited Over a Woman...

who my competition was, so I wanted to outdo everybody. The party went well, but I never felt I was doing enough.

Another of my efforts resulted from James' enthusiasm for the fine meals he had in French restaurants on his trips to Europe. I took a French gourmet cooking course. I got very good at it, and for a period of about six months we had a gourmet dinner almost every night. One advantage of this cooking class was that it was held at a place where the children were cared for while the mothers attended classes. I later took a guitar course the same way. Since I tried to be "supermother," this kind of setup was very important to me. I usually fretted about getting babysitters. I worked hard at being a good mother, and I resented the small amount of attention James gave the kids. Even when he wasn't traveling, he spent very little time with them. I was concerned about his lack of involvement. I also felt if he were more involved with them he would be more committed to me and to our marriage.

James:

For about seven months I was really preoccupied with Lisa. I called her between visits and thought about her daily. We grew very close. At the same time, we retained a lot of that initial excitement. We didn't take each other for granted like a lot of married partners do when they get comfortable with one another. Of course we didn't have to deal with the day-to-day details of living together that sink a lot of otherwise good love relationships. When we came together we were about as free as you can get, so we were able to devote ourselves to simply enjoying that time. And our times together were infrequent enough so that we never got the feeling we completely knew each other. There was always a sense of exploring and discovering.

One other factor which kept our relationship exciting was Lisa's playfulness. She was very creative. She enjoyed smuggling wine, cheese, and fruit into the hotel in her purse. Frequently, when I arrived back at the hotel after a day's work, she would have a veritable banquet laid out. On one visit when I was feeling under the weather, I opened the door to find Lisa in the nude and the room half-filled with inflated balloons. It was her way of lifting my spirits. It worked.

At one point I became worried that Lisa was giving up too many possibilities at school and committing too much time to me. It's not that she made any demands. She never did that. I just found it hard to believe she could always be available when I called. She had to have a pack of guys panting after her. We talked about it and she assured me everything was OK. She did date at school—mostly her professors. She told me about her dates in general, but was wise enough not to say too much. I was determined not to feel any jealousy, but I don't know that I could have avoided it if I had known details about her other relationships.

I talked frequently with Lisa about Peggy and the kids. I think I did it partly as a reminder to both of us of my commitment, and also because it was an important part of my life. She seemed genuinely interested. She frequently asked questions about how it was going, but she never once said anything disparaging about Peggy or our marriage.

Peggy:
Because of my fear and suspicion about James' traveling, I quickly adopted a strict rule: "Never deny him sex anytime he wants it." I figured I'd be inviting him to get it somewhere else if I did. I tried to make sure we had a good session of lovemaking the night before he left on a trip. Then when he got home I waited to see how anxious he was to make love—as if I could somehow measure whether or not he'd had sex while he was away. The saddest part of this was that I was performing in bed for his benefit—with no thought as to what I wanted.

Actually, all I wanted was for him to want me. I was so uptight as to whether I was pleasing him, I seldom had orgasms anymore. I did a good job of pretending passion

When a Man Gets Excited Over a Woman...

and faking orgasms. I was so totally geared to focusing on his feelings for me that I honestly don't know what I felt for him.

Night after night I'd lie very still in bed, hoping he'd want me. It was like checking a barometer to see where I stood in his favor. I read books on sex and tried everything I could think of to keep him happy and satisfied. I thought our sex life would make a big difference in his actions. I had bought the myth that "if you keep him sexually satisfied at home, he won't look for it somewhere else." Lack of good sex at home is often given as the reason (excuse) for an affair. I had no idea how false those ideas were at the time. My later understanding of the way this actually works is that poor sex at home may encourage affairs, but good sex at home won't necessarily discourage them.

My worry about James having affairs was something I went to great lengths to hide from our friends. Anytime the subject of his traveling was discussed, I'd say, "He tells me all about his trips. I don't worry. I trust him completely." I tried to appear confident of his faithfulness. I needed to present this front to protect my pride.

I think this false front is typical. Lots of women sense their husbands are having an affair, but hope they're wrong. Others know for sure...but pretend they don't. Some women protect themselves from dealing with it either by refusing to acknowledge the possibility—or by clearly telling their husbands they don't want to know about it. Anything seems easier than facing the truth. Perhaps that's because so many women feel compelled to file for a divorce when they discover an affair. That's what I was trying to avoid. I kept hoping I was wrong so I wouldn't feel pushed into getting a divorce. It took a lot of rationalizing to hold onto this hope.

One time when James came home from a trip I found a long, blond hair in his suitcase. I'm a brunette. My first impulse was to cry and scream. I Knew. But I had to find a way to deny it. I wracked my brain to find a way to explain away my fears. I finally recalled that the wife of one of the men he worked with went on the trip—and she had a blond wig. I tried to tell myself maybe it was hers. I ignored a lot of obvious clues in trying to reassure myself.

One thing I simply couldn't ignore was the fact that James had completely stopped saying, "I love you." While this hadn't been something he said every day, he'd always been comfortable with saying he loved me. I thought it might be part of his growing sophistication—that he felt it was too sentimental or something. I didn't know why, but I knew it hurt. Sometimes I said, "I love you" and waited to see how he would respond. All I usually got was a hug or a "me too" at most—like it was awkward or embarrassing. Sometimes he didn't respond in any way, and I'd really feel discouraged. At those times I'd tell myself I absolutely would not say it anymore until he did. But after waiting for awhile, I always broke down and said it again. I couldn't bring myself to ask him directly to say he loved me. I felt if you had to ask, it somehow didn't count. He had to want to.

James:
I had not intentionally stopped telling Peggy I loved her. In fact, when she first told me that I hadn't said I love you during a four-year period, I didn't believe her. It didn't fit with the way I felt. I think it resulted from the general restrictions I put on my emotions during that period in order to keep things sorted out rationally. Also, I was preoccupied with my career.
One of my faculty assignments was to be on the staff of an intensive week-long lab that formed the first week of an eight-week residential program for executives. The participants were upper level managers from business and government—all male and practically all from out of town. The pace of that first week didn't allow much time for exploring the city, so another faculty member and I established a tradition of giving them a guided tour on Friday night of some of the more interesting night life. We'd start with a group dinner and then make about seven or eight

When a Man Gets Excited Over a Woman...

stops in bars and night spots in the area. It had generally been a night of fellowship and drinking—a good release from the intensity of the week. I'd noticed on past tours that some of the men were a lot more interested in the spots where there were more single women, but in my innocence I hadn't thought much about it.

This year it was different. My innocence was dwindling. There was no need to beat around the bush. A little camaraderie was fine, but what most of the men wanted to know was where they could find a woman. So I conducted the tour accordingly. I used to focus on the entertainment and the quality of the drinks. Now I tuned in to the quality of the single women and the ease with which you could make contact. I didn't learn all that from Lisa, and I was still not into picking up women in Pittsburgh. It's just that I'd developed a different way of looking at women and night spots after entering the world of affairs.

I was aware it was getting late, but since I had no intention of getting involved with a woman myself that night, I wasn't concerned. I was prepared to give Peggy a detailed description of all the places we visited. And I expected her to accept it without question. What a blockhead I was.

Peggy:
I knew the round of night spots where James usually went on the tour, and I knew most of them closed at twelve or one o'clock. On this particular night I was waiting up for him, as usual, but he didn't come home at midnight. At 1:00 a.m. he was still out. I got more and more anxious. By 2:00 a.m. I felt sure he'd come in the door any minute, so I sat and stared out the window, tensely waiting and watching. I kept imagining I could hear the car—but still he didn't come. I began to feel desperate. I considered calling the wife of another man who worked with him in the course, but I thought, "What if her husband is home in bed and James is

out with another woman? What can she say? What will they think?" My pride kept me from calling.

By 3:00 a.m. I began to think he'd either been killed in a wreck or had disappeared altogether. I couldn't imagine he wouldn't have called if he were going to be that late. The next hour was like a dream—I was so distraught I couldn't think straight. At 4:00 a.m. he finally came home. When he walked in the door, I collapsed in his arms. I was totally exhausted from waiting and worrying for so long.

When I could regain enough strength to talk, I asked, "Why were you so late? Why didn't you call?"

"I didn't call because I thought you'd surely be asleep, and I didn't want to wake you."

He calmly explained that after visiting all the regular spots, they went on to a new one that was open until 4:00 a.m. and some of the guys wanted to stay. Of course, this was all connected with his work—which meant I shouldn't complain. He always managed to sound so logical; I didn't know what to think anymore.

Every day became a struggle. My emotions began getting the best of me. I was upset and depressed most of the time. James suggested I go to a psychiatrist to find out what was wrong. I already knew what was wrong. I was afraid he was having an affair—and I didn't know what to do about it. I couldn't bring myself to confide in anyone, but I had to do something. I decided to start keeping a journal—where I could pour out my feelings and try to get some control over them.

I feel so scared and alone. But I can't talk to anybody. I don't want them to feel sorry for me. And I certainly can't talk to James. If I asked him point-blank, I know he would deny it—whether or not it's true. If I'm wrong, I don't know what he might do. But if I'm right, I don't know what I would do. I don't really think I could handle it. I'd have to get a divorce to save my pride. But how could I ever make it alone with the kids? I've lost whatever confidence I once

When a Man Gets Excited Over a Woman...

had. I feel helpless. I certainly couldn't go home to my folks. I'd feel like too much of a failure. And I'd die of embarrassment.

But I don't think I can stand much more of this. I feel like I'm falling apart. I've got a pit in my stomach and a lump in my throat so I can hardly breathe. My head aches. I feel weak most of the time, with practically no energy. I've lost my appetite. I have a constant metal taste in my mouth that I can't get rid of.

I can't bring myself to believe all this. Affairs seem as unreal as car accidents or cancer. Yes, I know these things happen—but not to me! I know I've been trying to deny my suspicions. I've been trying to brainwash myself into thinking I might be wrong. All the time I've spent analyzing James' words and actions has really been aimed at looking for reassurance—not for finding the truth.

The writing seemed to help a little. At least it kept things from slipping around in my head quite so much. But it didn't eliminate my fears. Nothing could really do that. I just decided to do the best I could each day—and keep writing in my journal at night.

Spring finally came, and with it some important changes in our lives. We'd joined a new racquet club built during the winter in one of the suburbs of Pittsburgh. We decided to buy a house near the site of the club. I didn't feel very good about the financial stretch of buying a house, but I thought it might be a good thing for our marriage. It seemed more stable than renting.

James was in Europe when the time came to settle the closing. He left me a blank, signed form to use in finalizing the arrangements. We had never bought a house before, but I managed to handle it. I wanted James to think I was capable. I relished opportunities to show him how well I could manage. I loved it when he wrote me from Europe saying he really felt good that I could take care of things so well while he was away. I didn't realize at the time that this also took away some of the pressure of worrying about me and freed him to give more attention to his affairs. This was one of many situations where my efforts worked in opposition to the purpose I had in mind.

I was very good at self-defeating activities. I established a habit of giving too much and feeling bad about it. I resented James' traveling, but he made it difficult for me to say anything. He'd say, 'The traveling is part of my job. It's just as tough on me to make these trips as it is on you to have me gone so much.' I saw I might as well quit fighting it. It was getting me nowhere. I decided to try to be helpful and understanding instead. I did all his packing for him. I even said since we couldn't both go, I was glad he could go and share it with me. But I was lying through my teeth.

James:
The trip to Europe Peggy referred to was a two-week business trip. Most of it was spent in Geneva where I was coordinating a meeting with a group of managers from several European countries. I devoted about four nights to trying to make it with a young American girl in the motel where we were staying. It wasn't working, so another guy and I drove up to Megève to try our luck in some of the dance spots there. We met two Canadian women on a ski vacation and had a great time dancing and making love most of the night. After about an hour's sleep we drove the ninety minutes back down to Geneva just in time to shower, have breakfast, and begin our 8:30 a.m. working session. We should have been half dead; but there's something energizing about a new affair, and we both felt very much alive.

We had made arrangements to meet them again that night, so when we finished work about 6:00 p.m., we changed into casual clothes and set out again for the mountains. It was another fun evening. That should have been enough for reasonable people, but we did it again the third night—this time taking about three hours to drive up to Megève in a heavy snow storm. I was reminded of an old

When a Man Gets Excited Over a Woman...

saying, "When a man gets excited over a woman, his brain moves down below his waist." We were living proof of it, but we had a ball.

I flew back to the states the following day and spent the night in New York City with Lisa. I was dead on my feet. I was feeling the lack of sleep plus the jet lag. I managed to get through a lovemaking session, but for the first time since I'd been seeing her, I fell asleep early. It was unfortunate because she was into some stuff at school that she needed to talk about. I think she took it as a clear sign that it didn't make sense for her to count on me as much as she had in the past.

I'd found it easy to engage in the new affair in Europe. There seemed to be even less risk of being found out, and as long as I couldn't be with Peggy or Lisa, why not? I didn't go through any mental gyrations this time. It just seemed like the natural thing to do.

Peggy:
When James got back from Europe, everything was set for our move. We'd been married almost twelve years, and this was our first house. It was quite a thrill. But a bigger thrill for me was a statement he made shortly after we moved in. He said, "I can't think of anything more I want out of life except more time to enjoy it." I took this to mean he was very satisfied with his life—and with me. It never occurred to me the reason for his satisfaction was that he had the best of both worlds—a wife at home and lovers too. I'd thought only in terms of me or someone else. I'd assumed that involvement with another woman meant he didn't love me. So I took his statement to mean he did love me—even though he still wasn't saying the words "I love you."

This temporary optimism had a positive effect on me. I looked and felt more alive. In keeping with this new spirit, I cut my hair short. I threw myself into the work around our new house. We had a big yard, and I bought a lawn mower and added mowing to my other responsibilities.

BEYOND AFFAIRS

We also became involved in the racquet club, and that took a lot of my time. James and another man were supposed to be in charge of the committee to establish the tennis program and work with the pro. They both traveled a lot, so we two wives handled most of the tennis program that first summer. I also began playing tennis again after many years away from it. I'd been a good player growing up, but I'd virtually quit playing when we married.

Our house was not far from the club and there was no clubhouse, so we entertained a lot. We had parties or informal get-togethers almost every weekend. We had a more active social life than ever before. I generally felt good about this, but I did have trouble with the social kissing. The group we socialized with was into greeting each other with a kiss. I'd never been comfortable doing this myself—and I certainly wasn't comfortable with James doing it.

My real fear was that he might be privately involved with another woman. Since I wasn't willing to say that to him, I focused on this social kissing as a way to get at my concerns. I'd say things like, "Your kissing other women is embarrassing to me. It makes me look foolish." I thought by telling him how I felt about his behavior in these public situations I could somehow influence his private actions. He invariably responded with statements like, "That's ridiculous. Most of our friends do the same thing. You're the one who needs to change."

When I finally realized I wasn't going to change him, I began to try to change myself. It took a long time to get up my nerve. I finally managed to join in, but I continued to feel uneasy about this whole ritual for quite some time.

James:
In the spring of 1967 I had begun to spend several days each month in Washington, D.C., coordinating a research project on the impact of computers on managers. I met two people in the course of that work who had a significant influence on me. The first was Frank, a man my age who

When a Man Gets Excited Over a Woman...

was the most reckless chaser I had ever known. He had all the essential credentials for the fast track in the world of affairs. He was good-looking, athletic, smooth, successful, and becoming more successful all the time. He moved in the right circles in Washington—being on a first name basis with lots of people in high places. He was a workaholic, but a very productive one.

At the time I met him, he had his wife and kids comfortably situated in Maryland. That made it convenient for him to "work" late and even stay overnight in Washington three or four nights each week. His job was clearly an important one and he was doing it well. His wife would have had to be crazy to question his dedication and long hours of work. Or would she? The reality was that Frank was in his second year of an intense affair with his secretary. He was also open to making it with any other woman he could corner for five minutes. He traveled extensively and had semi-regular relationships going in several other cities. He was living the fastest life I had encountered. I thought it was bound to lead to trouble, but in some ways I admired him and wanted to be like him.

The other person who became important to me in Washington was Marge, a secretary for one of the men who reported to Frank. With Frank's blessing and encouragement I began an affair with her in May, 1967. She was single, twenty years old, and still living with her parents. On our first date I agreed to pick her up at home. Driving to her house it occurred to me for the first time I would probably meet her parents. Marge knew I was married, but we hadn't discussed how to handle that with them.

Sure enough, her mother met me at the door. I was nervous as hell. It's not that I expected her to ask me point-blank, "Are you married?" It just seemed crazy. In my wildest dreams, I'd never imagined myself as a married man picking up a young single woman and passing the time of day with her parents. I didn't want to lie, but the question was, could I tell them enough about myself to satisfy their curiosity without giving away that part of my life. I made it through that first meeting without any obvious problems. When I realized later that all the time I was talking to them I was wearing my wedding band, I really felt foolish. I made a decision right then to remove my wedding ring at the beginning of trips and replace it before going home.

Even with my ring in my pocket, I still felt damn uncomfortable chatting with her parents each time I picked her up. I kept telling myself it was crazy; but the sex was great, and the old saying was operating again. My brain had descended below my waist. About three months into this affair, I forgot to remove my ring before picking Marge up. I noticed it as she was introducing me to another of her relatives who was having dinner with her folks. I don't think anyone else saw it, but it shook me so much I decided to stop wearing it altogether. It was certainly risky in this situation, and I also reasoned that it would inevitably interfere in some future affair. I figured Peggy might question my not wearing it, so I prepared some weak reasons that I thought might satisfy her. My perceptions and thinking processes were now so distorted by my infatuation with affairs, I was unable to see her real reaction.

Peggy:
I was shocked when James announced he wasn't going to wear his wedding ring anymore. He said it turned on his finger and bothered him. He'd been wearing it for twelve years, and there was no way I could believe it had only now started bothering him. I thought he must be taking it off so he could pretend he wasn't married when he was traveling. But I wasn't willing to risk accusing him in case I was wrong. Considering the way he always presented such an above-it-all posture of himself in relation to such things, I felt sure he would deny it anyway. I was constantly confused by conflicting messages I got from him.

About this same time he encouraged me to pursue my longtime interest in music. He said, "I don't want you to

When a Man Gets Excited Over a Woman...

devote yourself completely to me. Someday you'll resent it if you sacrifice everything for me." I thought he just wanted to distract me from watching him too closely. I was afraid to do anything on my own that took away from my total commitment to him and the kids. I felt I'd surely lose whatever chance I might have of saving our marriage.

In my desire to please him, I rented a piano and started working on my music again. I'd done lots of singing throughout my school days. I was "local girl singer" in the small town where we grew up. I'd studied piano for twelve years. But I had given up most of this when we married. I only allowed myself a few excursions back into that world. I performed in a couple of college productions and briefly tried my luck at singing in New York when we were living in Connecticut, but it had been eight years since I'd done any performing at all.

Even though I loved singing, I wouldn't have pursued it then if James hadn't encouraged me. I was strictly doing it because he wanted me to. A couple of months after I began practicing, a prominent showman in Pittsburgh held a public audition. I decided to try out. I'd seen some of his shows and thought I might do pretty well, but I did better than I expected. As I was leaving the audition hall he sent someone after me to ask if I'd like to appear in an industrial show he was planning.

I could hardly wait to share the news with James. He was in a nearby town playing in a tennis tournament. The tournament was ending the next day, but I expected him to be coming home that night. He decided to spend the night and watch the final matches, so I had to tell him my news on the phone. I thought he'd be proud of me, but he wasn't particularly impressed. Even when he came home the next night, he showed very little interest in my success. I got the feeling that anything I did was less important in his eyes than anything he was doing, so he couldn't get very excited about it.

BEYOND AFFAIRS

The show took place a couple of months later. It was being put on for one large company. At the last minute the producer said we could invite our families to come if we liked. When I called James at home, eager for him to come, he said he shouldn't—his presence might make me nervous. I was terribly disappointed.

I now realize how much better it would have been if I hadn't used so much energy trying to please him. I should have taken pride in myself and my accomplishments and not depended on him to make me feel OK. I think women have traditionally been guilty of allowing men to determine their self-image. We've sold ourselves short by thinking our worth depends on the approval of the man in our life. That's exactly where I was. This caused me to miss a lot of chances to get a clearer sense of my own ability and worth as a person, separate from him. It also severely limited my enjoyment of life. Ironically, this dependency made James less approving than he might have been if I'd been a more independent person. I was far from independent. I functioned like a satellite around his world—always reacting to whatever situation he presented.

One situation I dreaded in particular was the office Christmas party James' work group held annually...without spouses. This year it was even worse that usual. We'd planned to go to dinner after the party. He was running so late I began to wonder if we'd still go, but I knew better than to call the office. I never questioned him or checked up on him like that. The wife of one of the other guys did call. Her husband told her he'd be home when he got there and she shouldn't call and bug him. She immediately called me to talk about it. While we didn't admit it to each other, I think we both felt anxious. I imagined all kinds of wild things happening—in keeping with my stereotypes about office parties.

When James finally came home, he'd obviously had a lot to drink. We did go to dinner with two other couples. One of the guys, who'd also been at the party, was so drunk he

When a Man Gets Excited Over a Woman...

passed out during dinner. This just reinforced my suspicions about the party being wild.

James:

Yes, Virginia, office Christmas parties are as wild as people say they are—at least some of the time. By Christmas, 1967, I was deep into outside relationships. It was clear that Karen, a woman at the university, was eager to start an affair with me. I was attracted to her, but had resisted becoming involved for two reasons. I'd seen the complications of work-related and in-town affairs, and I wanted to avoid that. Also, I was still seeing both Lisa and Marge. I didn't feel the need for another ongoing relationship, and I was pretty sure that was the kind she'd want.

So there I was at our Christmas bash, feeling good about life and feeling very content to enjoy drinking and dancing. We were a hard-working group and we frequently socialized together, so we got loose rather quickly. Late in the party I found myself in my office with Karen. Honestly, I didn't design this one. As the saying goes, she was all over me. I didn't offer much resistance. With a couple of drinks (and my brain below my belt), my reasoning went like this. "There's not much I can do about this—it's inevitable. All the guys in the office already know I cat around and we can probably keep the other women from finding out."

With a chair propped against the door (it didn't have a lock on it), we had a frantic screw on the carpet. I had a vague awareness I was already late to pick up Peggy for a dinner engagement. I figured I could blame my lateness on the office party being slow to break up. After all, I was one of the hosts, and it wouldn't look good if I left early. Of all the crazy things I did in those years, this has to rank close to the top.

BEYOND AFFAIRS

Peggy:
When I finally got through Christmas, there was the New Year's Eve party to contend with. I dreaded the party because I knew there would be a lot of kissing at midnight. I did a lot of worrying about who James might kiss and whether it would be an excuse to really kiss someone he was attracted to, or heaven forbid...involved with. Perhaps these are the kinds of jealousies I should have overcome at age sixteen, but I was terribly insecure. Every situation having anything to do with James and other women was an ordeal for me.

I got so worked up over my fears, I actually became sick at my stomach. This inadvertently (or maybe subconsciously) worked in my favor, because his concern for me kept him by my side at midnight, comforting me.

What a shame I was so incapable of enjoying anything. I was only interested in keeping him in line. I didn't even try to have fun—only to put on a good front by pretending to be enjoying myself. James became irritated at any displays of jealousy (since he set himself up as being so trustworthy); so I got very good at appearing to be totally involved in another conversation or activity while still being plugged into him like radar, conscious of every move he made.

It had become second nature for me to be insecure and jealous. I saw all women as potential competition. I think this attitude is all too common, much of it beginning when we're little girls. From our earliest experiences with what's expected of us, we find ourselves competing with each other—usually for the attention and approval of the opposite sex. This competition is a hindrance to freely sharing our feelings with each other.

I was too insecure to talk to another woman about my fears. This was really unfortunate. Sharing my worries with a close friend might have helped enormously. But James was friendly with all the women I knew, and I didn't know who I could trust. I was suspicious of almost every woman he came in contact with.

When a Man Gets Excited Over a Woman...

James:

I'd like to take full credit for having the good judgment not to get involved with any of Peggy's friends. The truth is I can only take partial credit. The rest goes to luck. I knew the risk was higher in messing around with friends. So I never actively pursued any. However, we had two or three friends that I was very attracted to. I identified them as likely candidates. At parties I communicated my liking for them in what I hoped were subtle ways, but I never went so far as to say, "Let's get it on." I'm lucky one of them never actively pursued me. Based on my track record, I wouldn't have resisted.

Peggy:

James and I spent New Year's Day painting our living room ceiling in preparation for putting the house up for sale. He'd decided to accept a position at a school in Rochester, New York, and we'd be moving to Rochester in May. This would be just one year after buying our house. But I felt pretty good about the prospective move. I always held out hope that any change might be for the better.

There was one change I hadn't counted on. James suddenly stopped painting and said, "Why don't we have another baby. I'd really like another child." At that moment I could have fainted. Nothing could have shocked me more. Here I'd been wondering if our marriage was going to hold together—and he was happy as a lark, suggesting we have another baby. This kind of thing kept me constantly confused about my suspicions. How could he talk this way if he were involved with someone else?

At first I thought, "Oh no! Even if I could get pregnant right away, our youngest would be almost five when the new baby was born. Just at the time when he'd be going to kindergarten I'd be staying home with another baby." I was afraid my being restricted at home with the kids had been a factor in James' growing away from me with his work and travel.

BEYOND AFFAIRS

Actually, I had wanted to have three children originally. But I'd wanted to have them two years apart so I wouldn't be home with preschoolers for too long. After we had a girl and a boy, James decided he didn't want another child. So I'd revised my thinking to go along with his wishes.

Now he'd changed his mind again and decided he did want another child. You'd think that on this one issue I might have stood up to him—but I didn't. I thought this must mean I'd been wrong to doubt him. I saw this as a sign he was committed to me. And I saw another child as possibly strengthening that commitment. I'd bought a lot of myths.

I finally said "yes" to having another baby and stopped taking the pill a couple of months later. At this point I felt much more secure in our relationship. The next four months were busy with selling the house and preparing for the move.

James:

I continued seeing Karen after our fling at the Christmas party. My guess about her had been right. She did want a regular thing. She lived in an apartment on the opposite side of town from where we lived. It was an area I could never imagine Peggy going, so I felt pretty safe in meeting her there. I played indoor tennis not too far from her place every Friday evening, so we developed a routine of meeting in her apartment for two or three hours before my tennis game.

I'd told her I'd be reluctant to take much time away from Peggy when we started the affair and that I wasn't available for a permanent relationship. I think she still hoped I'd fall in love with her and leave Peggy, although I never gave her any indication it was a possibility. I was generally honest with all the women I got involved with, and in this particular area I was consistently and scrupulously honest.

In talking with others, I've learned that many people are more honest in their extramarital affairs than they are in their marital relationships. There's a lot of irony in this. Believing our marriage is our most important relationship,

When a Man Gets Excited Over a Woman...

we seldom approach total honesty with our spouse. We're too fearful of the long-term consequences. In trying to build a close relationship we are actually creating distance every time we hold back or present ourselves as something we're not. In trying to protect ourselves and our partner from discomfort in the present, we are setting ourselves up for some real pain in the future.

It's much easier to be honest in an affair because we don't have to be concerned about long-term consequences. We have less at stake. Here's the irony of ironies. Sincerely intent on limiting our involvement in an affair, we present ourselves honestly to our illicit lover. The result is, we frequently develop more caring and intimacy than we bargained for. This surprises many a person in an affair. They honestly didn't intend to get deeply involved. But honesty is appealing and attractive. There's a sense of well-being that comes from being accepted for who you are without pretense. Very few seem to achieve that in marriage, but it's fairly commonplace in affairs. Of course, it's much easier to accept someone and be ourselves when there's not so much at stake. An affair can provide enjoyment for a little while, but marriage is forever!

There are many variations of honesty in affairs. Some people present elaborate facades in order to make contact, then drop them once the relationship has been started. Others maintain the facades throughout the life of the affair. In both cases the affair will tend to develop the same kinds of problems common to most marriages where dishonesty is the norm. There seems to be a snowball effect operating in both directions. One person's honesty stimulates an honest reply from another. On the other hand, dishonesty frequently prompts a dishonest response.

Marriages sometimes suffer from comparison with affairs on this dimension. Honesty in an affair may make a dishonest marriage relationship look too messy and complicated to clean up and lead some to give up too soon. But comparisons are deceptive. There's a certain make-believe quality to a good affair, whereas marriage is for real. In an affair we create a little space in our lives where we can really devote ourselves to physical and emotional pleasure. Knowing that the relationship doesn't carry over into other areas of our lives makes it easy to pour our energy into the time we do commit to it. It's as if we're saying, "Let's pretend these other areas of our lives don't exist. Let's just enjoy the time we have together without cluttering it with all the mundane problems of living." What a difference between that and the attitudes associated with the marriage vows most of us took. "For better or for worse, 'til death do us part." It's no wonder that a satisfying affair often makes marriage look like it's all "for worse." Many find out too late that ending a burdensome marriage to pursue an affair as their primary relationship doesn't really solve anything. When the affair becomes a full-time thing, it frequently takes on the same qualities the marriage had.

    I was learning something else in my affair with Karen. In-town affairs are too complicated. Out-of-town affairs usually have clear time limits based on one partner's travel. These limits are generally easier to accept than the arbitrary ones someone has set for an in-town affair. I was feeling pressure from Karen for more time, so I was relieved to bring this one to a natural ending when we moved to Rochester. I promised myself not to become involved in-town again.

4

First, The Game

Peggy:
Our move to Rochester in May of 1968 was the beginning of even more distance between James and me. What I'd hoped would be a better situation turned out to be worse. He showed me his new office one Sunday afternoon soon after we moved. Then he said, "You are never to come to the office or to call me at the office unless it's an emergency." I knew he was under a lot of pressure with the move. He'd even lost interest in sex for the first time in his life. I also realized men don't want to appear henpecked in front of other men. But his position seemed too harsh.

He made it clear that he was earning the money and I had no right to interfere with whatever he thought was necessary for his work. He used his role of provider as the ultimate proof of his importance. I felt so insignificant—like a nuisance to be tolerated. Whenever there was a conflict between my needs and his, or my problems at home and his at work, he always pulled rank with his money-earner role as deserving priority. It wasn't difficult for him to convince me. I'd bought society's standard that earning money signified importance and power. Being a housewife and mother was given lip-service, but it wasn't valued by society in the same way.

I felt completely powerless and helpless. I didn't value my opinions because I didn't value myself. I went into every disagreement with James assuming I'd be shown where I was wrong. I made it easy for him to take advantage of me. And he did.

He said I was not to expect him home at any specific time. His days were hectic with classes and meetings and he never had time to himself until after 5:00 p.m. He wanted to relax and work quietly, without checking with me about when he'd be home. I knew he was working hard, so I accepted whatever he said. After all, he was the important person earning money for us.

James:
This posture of "don't bug me at the office" was serving a couple of purposes for me. I thought it was useful to keep a sharp separation between my home and work life. It gave me a greater sense of freedom and I figured it would make it easier to keep my affairs more distant from Peggy. The other factor was purely chauvinistic. If your wife called you often or showed up frequently at the office, the implication was you were henpecked or at the least "tied down." A few guys at the office were the butt of constant jokes on this account. It seemed they and their wives couldn't do anything on their own without checking with each other. In my effort to avoid that extreme, I overreacted in the opposite direction. I wanted to show without a doubt that I was my own person, not controlled by Peggy. I never guessed that it had such a strong impact on her—another example of my insensitivity to her feelings.

First, The Game

My vow to avoid in-town relationships lasted for the entire summer after our move. It took some deliberate self-control. The first week on campus, I met a very attractive woman named Terry. She turned men's heads in every room she walked into. It was obvious we were attracted to each other from our first meeting. Whenever I saw her, I was careful to maintain a very polite, professional posture. During the latter part of the summer my resistance began to break down. We both started communicating our feelings with eye contact. We didn't talk about it, but our way of looking at each other left no doubt in either of our minds about what we wanted to do.

Finally, in September my resistance was completely gone. As Terry was about to leave the university late one afternoon, I asked her to stop by my office. When she came in, I got up to close the door. I knew my voice was going to shake when I spoke. I was confident of the way she felt about me, but I was still nervous as hell.

"You know I find you very attractive."

"Yes, I know."

"I'd like to have a drink with you, but I wouldn't want to stop there." "When did you have in mind?"

"Now."

"Let's go. I thought you'd never ask."

"Are you sure you can handle it?"

"I'm sure."

We walked to a nearby bar and took a booth in a nice, dark corner. I don't know why we actually went to the bar. We wanted each other so badly we could taste it, and we didn't need any preliminaries. We ordered a drink and started to touch each other for the first time. It was electric for both of us. The three and a half months of denying ourselves had increased our desire. We didn't finish the drinks. Trying to appear calm, we almost ran from the bar to our cars, drove to her apartment, and screwed ourselves silly. This was the beginning of my longest and, in some ways, most intense affair.

BEYOND AFFAIRS

Peggy:
It's a good thing I didn't get pregnant. James was almost totally immersed in his work (and his affair). By the end of September I'd been off the pill for nine months, and my system hadn't picked up functioning on its own. I'd visited the doctor regularly and never knew from one month to the next whether I was pregnant or whether my system just wasn't geared back up after going off the pill. Even the doctor thought I was pregnant at one point. Finally, he determined I wasn't pregnant and managed to get me regulated again. We stopped our efforts to have another child. James had lost his earlier interest in having another baby. He didn't even seem to have much interest in the two children we already had. Many days he didn't even see them. At ages six and four, they were frequently in bed when he got home.

In addition to not knowing when he would be home, I never knew whether or not he'd have had dinner. He said he sometimes liked to go out for a quick dinner and go right back to work. I tried to keep food I could cook quickly if he came home late without having eaten. I didn't feel I had the right to rebel against this situation. I bought the idea that since he was taking care of me financially, it was my duty to do whatever he expected of me in my role of housewife.

James:
I'm ashamed of the way I used my "breadwinner" role to intimidate Peggy and get my way. I rationalized it at the time because there was an element of truth in the position I took. I was working hard, and I did work best when I wasn't on a fixed schedule. It also made it easy for me to spend time with Terry without having to account for my whereabouts. Any way you cut it, I was being unfair to Peggy. I was conscious of using that strategy to protect myself, but I never really stopped to look at what it was doing to her.

First, The Game

Peggy:

I did manage to feel pretty confident in a number of other areas that had nothing to do with James. I worked part-time at the nursery school that Andy attended and led the Brownie Troop Vicki was in. I also organized a playschool at the local tennis club, handling approval, support, budgeting, hiring, and construction of the playground. It felt good to be active, and it also took my mind off worrying about James.

I also did all the work around the house. I handled all our financial business (paying bills, doing our income tax), and all our social business (entertaining, buying gifts for friends and family, correspondence). But none of these maintenance efforts showed up as important. James' one contribution at home consisted of the woodworking items he made as a hobby. His work showed up in a special way while mine got taken for granted. Since my efforts didn't get valued as much by either of us, my self-esteem continued to suffer.

I think self-esteem (or a feeling of self-worth) is strongly related to the kind of attitudes you grow up with. Many women have been conditioned from the time they're little girls to stand on the sidelines and admire the achievements of boys. And boys learn very early to think of themselves as superior to girls. Fortunately, this is changing, but in the time and environment in which I grew up, I had a clear image of the role I was to play in life—and it was a support role. I always assumed I would get married, have children, and be a housewife. I did not, however, realize I would be considered less important and that it would feel so bad.

It did feel bad to be taken for granted. I felt like an old shoe, comfortable and dependable. Also, like an old shoe, I felt I was wearing down. I began to feel it was inevitable we'd eventually get a divorce. I felt too unimportant in his life. He seemed to be going off in a completely different direction. It was clear we weren't going side by side the way

BEYOND AFFAIRS

I had imagined when we first got married. I think I was strongly influenced by the "happy ever after" Cinderella story. And in some ways I was still trying to make it come true. I kept looking for some signs of improvement.

One day in October James came home and said, "I just got it all set. We're going to Bermuda for a week. There's a tennis tournament I'll be playing in, and we can play mixed doubles if you want to." I was filled with mixed emotions. I liked the idea of taking a trip. Another couple was going too—a couple I liked very much. But I would have preferred to go somewhere—anywhere—alone with James, and without tennis.

I dreaded leaving the kids with a sitter. No matter how well I planned or how reliable a sitter I had, I always had pangs of guilt. Also, I invariably worried about money. We'd rented a house when we moved to Rochester, but we'd been hoping to find one to buy. A trip like this didn't seem practical when we needed to conserve our money for buying a house. I was generally the more practical of the two of us, but James said I was just too pessimistic. Anyway, the trip was planned, and I got busy preparing to go.

The closer the time came to leave, the more excited I became. James was to go ahead to New York for a couple of days on business and I was to meet him there to go on to Bermuda. The night before he left for New York I made a discovery that really knocked me off my feet. I had seen Terry at a number of university social functions and somehow sensed there was something between her and James. But I had discounted my feelings because I thought she was pretty attached to another guy. Then I found out she was no longer involved with the other man in the way I'd thought, so there was no way I could continue to deny my feeling that James was having an affair with her. This was the first time I'd suspected a specific woman. I'd had all kinds of fears about his traveling, but this was different. My anxiety would become an everyday thing instead of only during the times he was away. It was a very bad feeling.

First, The Game

After he left for New York I did a lot of thinking. I felt a need to fight back somehow. I decided to remove my wedding ring. Since he'd stopped wearing his ring a year earlier, I thought this was a fitting protest. He didn't even notice I wasn't wearing the ring until five months later.

When I got to the hotel where James was staying in New York, I was faced with an uncomfortable situation. I went to the desk, said I was James' wife, and asked his room number. I hadn't traveled much and was self-conscious about handling this, thinking the desk clerk might not believe me. After all, I reasoned, I didn't even have on a wedding ring. He didn't question me. He just picked up the phone, called James' room, and said, "Your wife is here. Is it all right to send her up?" Instead of saying, "Yes, I'm expecting her," James told him to send me up if I were good-looking. The desk clerk seemed to take it as a joke, told me the room number, and I went up. It wasn't funny to me.

I decided not to make an issue of it. Instead, I decided to make this the best week possible. I hoped James would see me in a different light away from my role at home. Things started well. Bermuda was beautiful. We arrived in the afternoon, and before we even unpacked, he wanted to make love. Sex in the daytime was such a luxury. With two small children, it's very difficult to have sex at home during the day.

The rest of the week was great as far as the weather, the tennis, and the entertainment were concerned. We laughed and played—riding motor bikes all over the place like a couple of kids—but we didn't have sex another single time the whole week. I couldn't understand why. I felt rejected. But I wasn't going to initiate sex because I used his desire for sex as an indicator of his feelings for me. I always waited for him to make it clear he wanted me. The rest of that week, it didn't happen.

I was desperate for information about his feelings for me, so I resorted to this way to test him. But I paid a price for playing these games. They made me look like the stereotypical wife who "isn't interested in sex." And by not initiating it, I put James in total charge of our sex life. He was then free to fit it into his schedule of outside sex as it pleased him. Even if I'd realized this, I don't think I could have forced myself to do otherwise due to my pride. Pride gets in the way of a lot of things. I couldn't imagine "forcing" myself on him if he didn't want me. Even if he hadn't rejected me, I needed to know he specifically wanted me when we made love.

We had done a few things "right" in our marriage from the beginning. We had always slept nude. And we made a point of going to bed at the same time and getting up at the same time unless some unusual situation prevented it. Despite this, we had not developed a habit of holding and caressing each other in bed without the expectation it would lead to intercourse. The extreme emphasis on intercourse leads many couples to interpret reaching to touch or kiss their partner in bed as a signal that intercourse is intended. This was the case with us, and it was even more exaggerated because of my efforts to test him on his desire to have sex with me. The results of this testing during the Bermuda trip really upset me because my hopes had been so high.

James:
I don't know how to explain my lack of interest in sex in Bermuda. I certainly wasn't seeing anyone else while I was there. I enjoyed the trip, and I'm sure we had ample opportunities. I simply can't remember what was happening with me. One thing I'm sure of—I didn't know Peggy was "testing" me by leaving it to me to initiate sex. I was getting plenty of sex. I came home many nights after a session with Terry, afraid Peggy would initiate some lovemaking. When she didn't, I was relieved. It never occurred to me to worry that something was wrong.

I can see now how this routine really created a lot of distance between us. Coming home from Terry, I'd make a

First, The Game

point of staying on my side of the bed and touching Peggy minimally so as not to arouse her sexually. I guess the more it happened, the more determined she became to leave it up to me. I was so caught up in what was happening with me that I never really noticed the game.

Peggy:

Meanwhile, there were other problems to deal with. Shortly after we returned we found just the house we wanted on a dead-end street near the tennis club. Having just spent money on the trip, it was hard to manage buying it then. We succeeded in making the arrangements and planned to move the day after Christmas.

On Christmas Eve I came down with the flu. I was sicker than I'd ever been in my life. I couldn't even get out of bed to go to the Christmas tree with the kids the next morning. James had bought me a silver halter dress for Christmas that was the sexiest dress I'd ever seen. As sick as I was, this boosted my spirits considerably.

Needless to say, we couldn't move the next day. But my dedication to duty led me to get out of bed a few days later to move. It was snowing and cold—and moving was a nightmare. A couple of unbelievable friends came and helped with the final packing of the kitchen stuff and the settling in at the other house.

Once we got moved, there was still a lot of work to do. I tried to do more than I felt like doing, but for several weeks I didn't accomplish very much. James had been supportive and compassionate when I was sick at Christmas, but he was getting irritated at my dragging around several weeks later. I knew how bad I felt, but I kept trying to get unpacked so he wouldn't be unhappy with me. That was one time I paid a high price for my unreasonable effort to please him. I had a relapse of the flu and the doctor sent me to bed for three weeks.

Finally, I recovered and got settled in the house in time to prepare for company. We had invited some friends from

BEYOND AFFAIRS

Pittsburgh to come visit us. When they arrived, I took them to meet James at work. When we got to the building where his office was located, I realized I didn't know which button to press on the elevator. I'd only been there once before, ten months earlier when we first moved. I felt stupid. It seemed terrible to be so excluded from his life that I didn't even know how to find his office.

I went into a period of doing lots of thinking and writing about our situation. I also started reading everything on couples I could find.

I can't tell James I don't trust him. But I've got to try to tell him some of my feelings. I have to find a way to make him understand how unhappy I am. It's finally dawning on me that he's happy with his life—and he assumes that if he's happy, I must be happy too. That word "happy" sounds so unreal. I don't even know what it means. I just don't want to be so UN-happy I've got a long way to go. I clearly can't count on James to make me happy. But surely I can find a way to keep him from making me so unhappy.

James was so involved in his affair with Terry that he wasn't aware of much of anything else—especially me.

James:
There were several reasons for the intensity of my affair with Terry. I've already mentioned one—the three and a half month period when we were both aware of our attraction for each other, but not doing anything about it. Another was the ease with which we could arrange to spend time together. Since we were both at the university, it was easy to see each other every day. We frequently managed to meet on Saturdays and Sundays too. Peggy knew I was writing up the results of a major research study and that it required a lot of extra work. I'd already developed the habit of working many nights and weekends on this project, so it was easy for

First, The Game

me to spend a good block of time with Terry under the guise of more work.

We had a typical routine. I'd go to her apartment about six o'clock. We'd make love, then lounge in bed with cheese and crackers and manhattans. After a couple of hours of listening to music and talking, we would usually have intercourse again. It's no wonder I stayed on my side of the bed when I went home to Peggy. I was getting all the sex I could reasonably handle. I probably saw Terry two or three nights a week for most of that school year.

This pattern satisfied both of us for the first few months. Hiding our relationship from others and being together for short times seemed a small price to pay for the enjoyment we were getting. In fact, both things add to the excitement of being together when you're starting an affair. As the novelty wore off, we began to resent the sneaking around we had to do to keep our affair concealed. We couldn't go out in public together, and we could never spend entire nights together. Four or five hours was usually the limit on our rendezvous. Understandably, this was more of an irritant to Terry than to me. After all, I was the one who had other commitments. She was free to do as she pleased. In an effort to be sensitive to her needs, I gradually took more and more risks in seeing her. Although I knew it was crazy, I eventually took her on an overnight business trip to a nearby town.

Peggy:

I was suspicious from the moment James left on the trip. It was to be a one-day program on Monday, but he drove over Sunday night instead of waiting until the next morning to go. He said he didn't want to have to get up early. I immediately suspected he was up to something—possibly with Terry.

That night and the next day seemed to drag by. I could hardly wait for him to get home. The program was to end at 5:00 p.m., so I figured even if he had dinner there, he should be home by 9:00 p.m. I began watching for him then, but hour after hour passed with no word. I got more and more upset. I finally went to bed about midnight and lay there listening for him. I kept imagining he might not come home at all. Then I'd worry that he'd been in a car accident. I was too nervous to stay in bed, so I got up again and waited.

He finally got home about 2:00 a.m. He'd obviously had a lot to drink, so I decided not to try to talk to him then. When the credit card statement arrived at the end of the month, I did talk to him about the size of the dinner charge from the first night of his trip. He said he'd eaten alone that night, but the amount seemed impossible for only one person. I was naive about lots of areas of travel and costs, but there was no way I could imagine one person spending that much on a meal in any restaurant, no matter how nice.

James:
Peggy's suspicions were on target. Terry and I had eaten at a very expensive restaurant and I used my credit card to pay the bill, as I frequently did on trips. I usually thought ahead and was ready with some plausible explanation in case Peggy ever were to question me. I had a standing agreement with a couple of my colleagues that we virtually always had dinner together on the road to cover such instances if necessary. This time I hadn't anticipated it. When Peggy asked about the size of the bill, I mumbled some lame excuse about having a lot to drink and what an expensive place it was. I knew at the time she wasn't buying it. No one in their right mind would have. I couldn't think of anything else to say in my panic, so I just clamed up. I did resolve to use more care in the future.

Peggy:
I couldn't avoid feeling he was lying. While there had been other times when I hadn't been sure he was being completely honest with me, this was the first time I felt he had lied outright. He usually just avoided discussing things that might put him in the position of telling a lie. And I

First, The Game

cooperated in this by not asking him questions that would force him into that position. Even in this instance, I didn't openly accuse him of lying.

I did talk to him about how it hurt me for him to spend so little time at home. I told him I felt I was losing touch with him. I told him about my writing therapy and the reading I'd been doing about marriage issues. I was able to do it in a very straight way, without being emotional or overly critical. I'd never been able to handle things this way with him. I'd always preferred to talk at night because it somehow seemed safer to talk about my feelings in the dark. I usually felt incapable of holding my own in a discussion with James. This time he seemed to understand my feelings. He was genuinely touched by the energy I was putting into working on our relationship.

James:

I'd been worrying about spending more time with Terry when I should have been concerned about Peggy-and me. I'd been stretched about as thin as any person needs to be stretched, by my own choosing. There had been a growing amount of tension between us. She wasn't getting enough of my time and interest. I was so preoccupied by my other involvements, I'd refused to face up to her discontent. I assumed my primary commitment to her was obvious and that it would be enough to carry us through. I now see my assumption was a poor one. I don't think our marriage would have lasted if I'd continued that way much longer.

The funny part is that for years I thought I had the best marriage of anyone I knew. The few problems I had with Peggy were small in comparison to those I saw in other marriages. Probably the thing that bothered me the most was her perfectionism. When we were entertaining people at home, Peggy would go to great lengths to have everything just right. If something didn't go right in her view, she would get upset and hassle herself for days about it. She would conceal it from whoever we were entertaining, so that wasn't a problem. I just felt it was unnecessary to spoil anyone's time, including hers, with what I viewed as "crying over spilled milk."

Peggy:
What James failed to see was that my role as wife and mother was my job—my work—in the way his role as a professor was his. I took pride in doing a good job. It was important that I be successful in my work as a homemaker. To him it was frivolous. But I knew that a lack in anything to do with the home, the kids, or the entertaining reflected on me—not on him. That was the nature of the role divisions we had bought into. And since we had divided things that way, my performance in my role was as important to me as his job performance was to him. But he didn't see it that way. He saw it as "crying over spilled milk." It's too bad we had such narrowly defined roles. We could have shared so much more of our lives with each other if we had been more open.

James:
During those years I didn't see Peggy as a resource in my teaching and consulting, so I didn't seek her help in those areas. I now know she could have been a powerful ally there, had I been open to it. I was too conditioned in seeing her as "just a housewife."
On all the important things, Peggy was giving me everything I wanted in our marriage. She was always there for me. She was basically supportive in everything I undertook. She was a significant asset in my social-professional life. It's difficult to be specific about the benefits that accrued to me in this area. They were intangible, but I clearly felt them.
There was an active social scene at both universities—frequently involving sit-down dinners and dancing. It was a definite plus to have a wife who was bright, attractive, a good conversationalist, and a good dancer. Peggy had all

First, The Game

these attributes in spades. I never had any concerns that she would do anything but enhance my image on any of these occasions. Maybe the best way to put it is that I collected some extra respect and esteem by virtue of having such a sharp, attractive wife.

Peggy's physical attributes have been important in our relationship. I've always found her physically attractive. I know other men have too. It's true that I was first attracted to her ass back in the ninth grade, but even then she had a well-proportioned figure. And she's always maintained it. She's been a good sexual partner throughout our lives together. I don't want to make her sound like "superwoman," but in truth, the above is an understatement. She's always been responsive and willing to experiment. And she's always taken care of herself in a way I've found sexually attractive. It was clearly not lack of good sex at home that caused me to start having affairs. I was getting everything I wanted from Peggy in that department—with the exception of complete novelty which was impossible for her to provide.

Another important thing about Peggy physically has been her general strength and good health. She's very feminine, but she doesn't shy away from good, physical work. She never has. That's enabled us to do a lot of physical things together, work and play, which many couples can't do. I valued this because of what it meant for her and me. She could stand on her own two feet and didn't need to call me every time a task required physical strength. Some very important parts of life are basically physical. You have to touch and taste them directly. Yet women in our society have been conditioned to see themselves as fragile—not capable of dealing with some of the more physical aspects of life. Peggy either escaped or overcame that conditioning.

We had developed very sharp role distinctions after the kids were born. I worked and provided the money. Peggy took care of the house and kids. And she was extremely competent at it. I never had to worry about that part of our lives and was free to put more energy into my work and hobbies (tennis and affairs). I thought everything was great. I realize now that I missed some rich parts of life in not having more involvement with the kids during that stage. I also realize it was an unfair burden to put on Peggy. But that's all in retrospect. At the time I thought I had the world on a string, and everything was as it should be. I was working hard. I was successful and providing well for Peggy and the kids. Therefore, I deserved my devoted wife and my tennis—and my affairs. Practically every man I knew would have given his eyeteeth to have the life I had. I see it differently now, but that's the way I thought at the time.

Peggy:
Many men get carried away with a sense of their own importance and the importance of their careers. Men have been conditioned to be success-oriented, so it's understandable. They often say, however, that they're committed to their jobs for the "sake of the family." Most men would be equally committed to their work if there were no family for whose sake they were doing it. This commitment to career usually has as many, or more, drawbacks for the family as it has advantages. It tends to create the kind of separation from family that leads to a husband and wife moving further apart. It's not the amount of time or energy spent on the job that determines this separateness, but the degree to which work life is not seen as relevant to home life—when they are kept in two neatly divided areas. When this happens, it's only a small step to separating other things as having nothing to do with home life. Sports and hobbies are usually included in this "separate world." Once this pattern is well developed in a number of areas, affairs are more likely to occur. It's a simple matter to keep affairs separate if other aspects of life are already seen as separate and having nothing to do with the family.

James had kept me pretty closed off in one little corner of his life for several years. But things took a real upswing

First, The Game

when he made a trip to South America in April of 1969. It had only been a few weeks since the trip that had stimulated some better communication between us. James called me when he stopped off in Texas on his way to South America. He said he'd been thinking about me ever since he left—especially thinking about our recent discussion. And he'd been reading the book I gave him on couples. He sounded more caring and loving than he'd ever sounded when he was away on a trip.

James:

It was true. Peggy had gotten my attention. But not to the point of causing me to change my ways yet. One of the most exciting short-term affairs I experienced occurred on the front end of this long trip to Texas and South America. I was scheduled to work in Dallas and Fort Worth on Thursday and Friday, fly to Cali, Colombia, on Saturday, and enjoy a free weekend there before beginning some business meetings on Monday afternoon.

Thursday afternoon I met a beautiful blonde at the motel in Dallas where we both were staying. She was sunbathing by the pool when I went out for a quick swim before dinner. I'd never found it easy to approach complete strangers and engage them in conversation. She was so attractive I decided to take the risk.

"Are you alone?" "Yes." "Do you mind if we talk?" "Go ahead."

I had just taken another step in the world of affairs—making a blind approach that sometimes works, but could get you in deep trouble.

Her name was Barbara. She was single and had just finished interviewing for a modeling job. She lived in Illinois and didn't know a soul in Dallas. Now I really started to feel excited—like the cat that just caught the canary. "Do you like to dance?" I asked, hopefully. "I love to," was her reply.

BEYOND AFFAIRS

"Why don't we have dinner and go dancing afterward. I know some clubs with good, live music.

She looked into my eyes for a long time and finally said, "OK." My heart was doing double time, but I tried to look cool as we agreed on when I would pick her up. After feeling a little tired and bored from the day's work, I now felt like I could swim about a thousand laps without stopping. There's nothing like a little positive anticipation to rejuvenate tired blood.

As Barbara and I drove to dinner, all I could think about was how I wanted to get in bed with her. What a waste it was to be going out. But first, the game. We went to a fine restaurant where the service was just right—slow and easy so it never seemed to interfere with our conversation. I told her about Peggy and the kids. She didn't seem too surprised at my being married, but she was puzzled by my honesty.

"How can you be here with me if you're so committed to Peggy?" she asked.

"There's no way I could be with Peggy tonight, so I might as well be doing something I enjoy. And I certainly am enjoying being with you."

"But what if Peggy finds out?"

"That's a chance I'm taking, but the likelihood of her finding out is really quite small. We don't know anyone in Dallas." "But don't you think it's unfair?"

"I don't see how it can hurt her as long as she doesn't find out. Of course it would hurt her if I flaunted an affair in her face, but I'm not about to do that," I replied.

"How would you like it if she went out with another man?" Barbara asked.

"I wouldn't like it if I knew about it. But if I were out of town so that the two of us couldn't be together and I didn't find out, how could it hurt me?"

It was easy for me to say this since I was pretty certain Peggy was not about to go out with another man. Barbara was not convinced by my logic. She didn't buy my treatment

First, The Game

of Peggy either, but in spite of herself she started to trust me because it was clear I was being straight with her.

Peggy:

James was right in feeling secure about my not being involved with another man. But women are not likely to be taken for granted like that in the future. Women like Barbara are more aware. As a wife it's unlikely she would be as dependent and trusting as I'd been. It's also unlikely her husband would assume her faithfulness in the way James did with me. Women will not be so naive in the future. Knowing what goes on in the world of affairs may lead them to either play the game themselves with their own "double standard" or insist on honesty and fairness. This will present a different challenge for the man who has thought in terms of doing his own thing while his partner is involved only with him.

James:

I was honest with my partners in affairs because I thought it was the best way to protect myself. I didn't want a woman calling me at home or at work, thinking I was single and available. And I didn't want to start a relationship under a false pretense such as being unhappily married. I figured sooner or later the truth would be known, and I didn't want an angry woman coming after me. What I didn't reckon with was the attractiveness of honesty. Beautiful women get so many "come-on's" from so many obvious facades that it's a relief when a man comes at them straight and clean without being pushy. At the very least they find it intriguing.

Barbara began to tell me about herself. She was twenty-one and had been involved for some time with an older man. He was on vacation in Europe and she was unhappy because he hadn't taken her along. Not because she wanted to go to Europe so badly, but because she took it as a sign that he wasn't really committed to her. She had come to Dallas on a whim. She wasn't really interested in becoming a model. It was simply a way to get away from things for awhile and maybe avoid feeling depressed about her lover.

She was a senior in college and lived alone in an off-campus apartment. My mind went to work immediately, calculating ways I could get to Illinois. And we hadn't even talked of anything happening yet. Everything felt right though. She was a solid, thoughtful person. She was being straight with me. I liked her. I let her know this with my eyes as we talked.

It was a good dinner. We covered a lot of ground in a short time. She told me how mixed up she felt about her love relationship, and I listened without judging or advising. Time passed quickly. As we left the restaurant to go dancing, holding hands felt very natural.

The first spot we tried had a good band so we settled in there for the evening. Barbara was an excellent dancer. Of course, I wasn't really interested in dancing. What I wanted was to get back to the motel and get into bed with her. But not knowing how to engineer that directly, I had hopes we could work up to it while dancing. We danced practically every number, but I was especially eager for the slow ones. They gave me a good opportunity to express how close I wanted to be to her and a chance to gauge her reaction. As it turned out, I couldn't get a clear indication of where she stood. She wasn't holding me off. But at the same time, she wasn't pressing her body against mine in a way that said, "Let's get on with it." On the way back to the motel, I asked her to come to my room for a nightcap. She declined. Now I was up against the wall. She planned to fly back home the next morning. I had hopes of persuading her to stay in Dallas another night, but I hadn't even broached the subject. When I said I wasn't ready to leave her, she surprised me by saying we could continue to talk in her room.

Once in her room, we began to kiss. At last I thought the issue of getting in bed was settled. But she surprised me again. She refused to go any further than kissing. I told her how badly I wanted to make love to her, but she said she

First, The Game

didn't know me well enough. She liked what she knew of me, but it wasn't enough basis for going further. We talked and kissed until about 2:00 a.m. I kept hoping she would change her mind, but she didn't.

I asked her to stay over another night. She looked tempted, but said she should get on back. When I pressed her, she admitted she didn't have to get back for any particular reason, but persisted in saying she wouldn't change her plans. When we finally parted, I had lots of mixed feelings. It had been a very enjoyable evening. But I felt unfinished. I respected her resistance to making love. She was paying attention to how she felt—not just teasing me. Nevertheless, it simply increased my desire to make love to her. So I felt good and I felt disappointed. But I still had hope.

I had to drive to Fort Worth early the next morning for four or five hours of work. I planned to be back in Dallas about 4:00 p.m. Before leaving, I slipped a note under Barbara's door. It read something like this:

Barbara,
Please stay over. I'll change my flight to late Sunday and we can have the weekend together. I want to kiss you a lot—all over. Hope to see you by the pool about 4:30 p.m.
Jim

Driving back from Fort Worth that afternoon, I was optimistic and fearful at the same time. I'd been distracted all day, wondering what her decision would be. If she stayed, there wasn't much doubt about what we would do. I was driving the speed limit, but the car seemed to be crawling. I finally reached the motel and went straight to the pool.

She was there! I felt light as a feather. With great self-control, I walked over to her. What I wanted to do was run. She saw me coming. "Hi." "Hi. I'm glad you stayed." "Me, too."

BEYOND AFFAIRS

The words don't sound like much, but we were saying it all with our eyes. I had left my room key with the note that morning, and she had already moved her things into my room. There was no need to rush anything now. I changed into my swimsuit. We enjoyed a leisurely swim and soaked up the last afternoon rays of the sun. It seemed natural to go back to the room and make love, which we did. It was very enjoyable for both of us, probably much better than it would have been the night before. Then, she would have been a half-hearted participant, not sure she wanted to be having sex with me. Today, she had clearly decided after thinking things through, and it made all the difference.

Knowing we had the weekend ahead of us, we explored each other carefully and thoroughly. It was a fine weekend. Lots of gentle touch, sharing, and lovemaking. We also found time to do some more dancing and a little sight-seeing on Saturday. It was one of those luxurious times when all we had to do was please each other. No time schedules and no deadlines. When we parted on Sunday we were both feeling high. She agreed I could call her if I ever got to Illinois. I was determined I would.

(I did manage a trip to Illinois about four months later. I had dinner with Barbara and we enjoyed an evening together, but there was no sex involved. She was still seeing her primary lover and was afraid making love with me at the time might confuse things. I wished it could have been otherwise, but I didn't push her. It was good just to be with her. In the year following, we talked several times on the phone, but we never did get together again.)

Having affairs in the double standard mode requires some weird thinking. There is no honest way to justify it. And yet, if you think of yourself as a person with integrity, you have to try. One of the ways I tried was to focus on the positive effects of my affairs. Sometimes I had to stretch a little to make myself believe they were really benefiting Peggy as well as me, but at times like this it seemed clear enough.

First, The Game

The weekend with Barbara left me feeling alive and vital. I had a deep sense of well-being and, at the same time, a feeling of boundless energy. I was in love with life. Flying down to Cali, I was aware of how much I loved Peggy. I know there seems to be a contradiction in my saying I was thinking about my love for Peggy right on the heels of an affair that was so enjoyable. It seems contradictory to me too, but that's what happened. I loved her throughout the entire period of all my affairs. I was never tempted to leave her and take up life with someone else. In different ways, each of my affairs caused me to appreciate our relationship anew.

In this instance I shared some of these good feelings with Peggy in the following letter. I cried as I wrote it. Not sad tears. Tears of deep emotion. I was getting in touch with how much I really loved her. And it shook me.

April 28, 1969

Hi Darling,

It was good to talk to you the other night although I find it strange that I am seldom able to express verbally the way I feel in those situations. For the last few days I've felt like I was going to burst open with love for you. I felt that way when we talked but I couldn't say it. I think part of the reason is related to the general constraint that seems to be part of the way I react to practically everything. The constraint serves me well in some situations but I don't like it in this one, and yet it's clearly not something I can turn on and off like a radio.

Aside from my frustration at not being able to express my feelings easily, I am surprised at the depth and power of my feeling for you right now. There has never been a time since our marriage when I didn't love you and I have generally felt that our relationship has grown over the years. Still, the feelings I am trying to describe now seem different. My love and my esteem for you seem to have taken some giant strides and I wasn't aware there was that much room for growth.

Of course I can ascribe some of my feeling to the effects of travel. Absence really does make the heart grow fonder. But I think the change started a few weeks ago—perhaps when you told me about your reading and the way you work through your own feelings by writing them down. That definitely had an effect on me. The knowledge that you were working that hard to make our relationship better increased my love for you and my esteem for you as a person. Reading the book on couples also had some kind of effect on me. I didn't completely understand it but I think it gave me a renewed appreciation for the value I attach to our relationship.

I am at the university now and I haven't finished all I want to say but I think you ought to have the message that I love you very much. Please tell Vicki and Andy how much I miss them and that I love them too. I wish you could all be with me. Must go now.

        Love to all,
        James

Peggy:

I could hardly believe the love James showed in this letter, especially since he hadn't said "I love you" for two years. He'd written me a couple of other letters during that time where he said he loved me, but never anything so overwhelming as this.

I was sure I must have been wrong about his affairs. I just knew he couldn't write something like this if he were involved with anyone else. That trip was the only one he ever made that I didn't worry at all. I was deliriously happy. The reason I had felt unloved and unimportant to his life, as he explained in his letter, was his general constraint in expressing himself. I felt this was finally the explanation for all my confusion about his feelings. I knew I couldn't go back and apply this explanation to all his past actions, but I

First, The Game

didn't even try. I just enjoyed a few days of peace from the pain I'd lived with for so long.

5

It's OK to Have An Affair If...

James:

After a few days in Cali, I flew on to Rio where I did something I never thought I would do. I hired a prostitute. I'd said many times in the past that I'd never pay a woman to go to bed with me. It didn't seem right. I'd always looked down on anyone who would "stoop that low." This was a good indication of how much I had changed without being aware of it.

I was alone in a Rio nightclub, feeling limited by my lack of knowledge about the culture and the language. I finally summoned enough courage to ask a young woman about twenty years old to dance. I was so naive it took about five dances for me to realize why she warmed up to me so quickly. In broken English, she finally got it across that she would be happy to spend some time with me for $20.

My past statements didn't even echo in my memory at that moment. Maria was very attractive. She didn't fit my stereotypical idea of a prostitute at all. Without really thinking about it, I agreed to the $20 and we left the nightclub. I wanted to go to my hotel, but she said she wouldn't be allowed to go in. She was dressed quite nicely, and I didn't believe the desk clerk would question us. She was very definite. That was out of the question. She went on to describe the arrangement she had with a place nearby, where she could rent a room for a couple of hours.

For the first time, I felt uneasy about the situation. I didn't like dealing with so many unknowns in a foreign city with no one to turn to. I had a quick fantasy that some joker would knock me in the head in the middle of intercourse and take my clothes and money. Once more, however, the old "brains to the genitals" saying proved true. I was too excited sexually to rationally evaluate the situation. I quickly convinced myself she looked too sweet to do anything like that. She led me to what looked like a small apartment house about five blocks from the nightclub.

At this point the action started to fit my stereotypes. After letting us into the foyer with her key, Maria knocked on what looked like an apartment door. A woman appeared who looked like a "madame" was supposed to look. She opened the door only wide enough to get a good view of us. Maria said she'd like a room for a couple of hours. The woman said sure, picked up a key from a nearby table, and handed it to her without another word. We took the rickety elevator to the third floor and opened the door to a small room with one bed, a chair, and an adjoining bathroom—the basics.

I still felt uneasy, but after assuring myself the door was locked and there didn't seem to be another way anyone could come into the room, I proceeded to undress. Watching Maria undress helped me forget my concerns. She was about 5'6" and had a beautifully proportioned body with lovely, clear skin. I was still not seeing her as a prostitute.

After several minutes of kissing and fondling, she asked, "What would you like me to do?" I was non-plussed. I'd never been asked that by a woman before. It struck me as kind of funny. I mean, it was ludicrous in the sense that anything she did was OK. But it was clear she was serious. She wanted to please me—give me my money's worth. She was indeed a prostitute. Not yet jaded, but serious about the "business" at hand.

I was still pondering the situation when Maria asked, "Like me to suck?" "Yes," I replied, a little sheepishly. I'd never been sucked before, but I was eager to find out what it was like. I found out in a hurry. It felt so good I had to stop her after a few seconds or it would have been all over—at least for awhile. After a pause I was able to take a few more seconds. Then we had intercourse, a little rest, and more intercourse. It was apparent I was satisfied ("spent" would be more like it). Maria then took away any doubt of her occupation by saying, "I've got to be getting back to the club now."

I shouldn't have been surprised, but I was. I was still basking in the pleasant feelings that come from good sex, and she was ready to look for another customer. We'd been together about an hour and fifteen minutes. The whole thing was interesting to me. I was involved, but at the same time I was observing as if I were participating in an experiment. This would later form part of my rationalization for going to bed with a prostitute. "It's not that I was that desperate for sex; I just wanted to see what it was like." Yeh, right. Rationalization is a fascinating process. The problem is when you're in the midst of doing it, it's not so easy to be aware of it.

I wanted to spend the night with Maria, but I was afraid to even ask how much that would cost. We dressed; she returned the key; I paid her $20; and we walked out into the now deserted street at about 1:00 a.m. I felt a little foolish at having been worried about being knocked in the head. I also felt good to be breathing the fresh night air. I took Maria back to the club and then walked alone on the beach.

BEYOND AFFAIRS

It was a beautiful night, and I felt great to be alive. I was awed by the experiences I was having. I wanted to drink in everything in sight—taste everything within reach. Rio was one of the liveliest, most exciting cities I'd ever visited. The natural beauty of the surrounding area was staggering. I was glad to be there and glad to have met Maria.

It's hard to describe, but the life I was living seemed to have a momentum all its own. I was going to places I'd never dreamed of and doing things I'd never imagined. It was exciting. I liked it and wanted more. I hated to go to bed at night for fear I might miss something. I never tired of seeing new places and learning about the different ways people live. I thought of Peggy often during these trips. I would have loved to share much of what I was doing with her. I guess my ideal would have been to have her with me during the days only. I really valued my "chasing" time at night. It was an integral part of the whole scene for me. In fact, I came to see it as an essential skill for a sophisticated traveler.

I saw Maria again the following night. The routine was similar. I picked her up at the club; we got the same room; and I got another $20 worth. This time I enjoyed it more. I was less preoccupied with what else might happen to me and was able to focus more on Maria. She was good at her profession. The whole experience left me with some new perceptions of prostitution—and the need to rearrange some of my beliefs and values.

Maria had effectively destroyed my previous mental image of a prostitute. She looked more like "the girl next door." Using my well-developed powers of rationalization, I reasoned, "How can a person that looks this wholesome be bad?" And, "What could be wrong with paying $20 to be with her? After all, if I picked up a 'straight' woman I would likely spend more than that on drinks and dinner."

I'd arrived at a new place in my way of looking at extramarital affairs. I had "progressed" through five stages to reach this point. In the beginning I maintained that I wouldn't get involved with another woman unless it was "meaningful" relationship. To me that meant there had to be more than sex. I had to enjoy being with the other person. We had to have some interests and values in common. I was adamant—even self-righteous—about these requirements. I mean, how could you think of yourself as a person with ethics and integrity if you went to bed with a woman just for sex?

Here's the way I had it "reasoned" out during this first stage. It's OK to have an affair if... (1) it's a meaningful relationship and you care about the other person, (2) it's out of town so you're not choosing the affair instead of your spouse, and (3) no one gets hurt. This meant you were discreet enough to keep your wife from finding out, and the other person understood your long-term commitment so she didn't get too emotionally involved. I never considered the possibility I could get too involved with another woman. I just couldn't or wouldn't conceive of it. I think it must be similar to the kind of denial most of us would make about the possibilities of becoming an alcoholic—before we know the facts about alcoholism.

I had barely grown comfortable with stage one when I felt the need to "broaden" my philosophy. I was traveling a great deal. I frequently found myself alone in a city where I couldn't be with Peggy or Lisa. Now the question became: "What harm could there possibly be in my seeing another woman in these circumstances?" All I had to do was define "meaningful" and "caring" a little more loosely, and I could still meet my three criteria. Beginning to have one-night stands marked my entry into stage two. I still believed it had to be meaningful. T really believed it. I'm writing about this now from quite a distance. It seems just as weird and far-fetched to me as it must to you. But it's an accurate description of the way I was thinking at the time.

I went progressively deeper into affairs. Stage three was maintaining two ongoing affairs in two different cities at the same time. Each stage involved a little more risk and required a little more finesse to keep all the balls in the air. I took pride in this. I saw it as a sign of sophistication and competence that I could have a good marriage and two affairs at the same time.

The fourth stage was having affairs in the same city where we lived. I'd stayed away from this at first because it was clearly more risky than an out-of-town relationship. Also, I couldn't think of any decent rationalizations for spending that time away from Peggy and the kids. Traveling made things simple. When I was away, I didn't have the choice of being with them. I had to travel in my work, so that was "out of my control." The best I could ever muster as a rationalization for an in-town affair was: "I need the variety—the change of pace. Peggy and I have a good thing, but if I spent all that time with her, we probably wouldn't get along nearly as well." That didn't sound too good, even to me. But I wanted the affair, so I bought it. I just didn't state it too loudly.

Being with a prostitute was the fifth stage in my progression. Of course, this is just one way of looking at affairs—the way it happened for me. Some men start with a prostitute and go the other way, finally ending up with a meaningful, long-term relationship. Others have such a negative experience with their first affair they don't go any further.

In talking with men who continue to have affairs of some sort, I've noticed two practically universal tendencies. The first is to take progressively greater risks. The initial affair is usually undertaken with plenty of trepidation. If all goes well, the next one involves less anxiety and successive ones even less. It's like learning any new behavior. We are very cautious at first. As we become comfortable with the change, it becomes a habit. The initial fears diminish and we are willing to risk at new levels. The risks are still as real as they were with the first affair. We just accommodate. Some men get so accustomed to them, they really don't notice after awhile.

It's OK to Have An Affair If...

The second tendency I've seen is rationalization. We seem to latch on to whatever explanation best suits our current situation. Sometimes the rationale gets lengthy and intricate. The more logical sounding, the better. Other times, it's as simple as, "I couldn't help it. I guess we're just animals."

Peggy:
The rationalizations men give for having affairs seem to be endless. Their versatility is fascinating.
—It's OK to have sex with a woman I really care for, but nothing casual...
—It's OK to have casual sex, but nothing serious...
—It's OK to go to a massage parlor, but not have "real" sex...
—It's OK if I'm out of town...
—It's OK if it's not in our social circle...
—It's OK if it doesn't interfere with my work...
—It's OK if the woman is single...
—It's OK because I deserve an occasional fling; I work hard and I've earned it...
—It's OK because my wife doesn't understand me (or doesn't appreciate me)...
—It's OK because it makes me a better lover...
—It's OK as long as nobody gets hurt...

Perhaps the biggest rationalization of all is—It's OK for me but not my wife. Many men who are actively engaged in affairs say they wouldn't stand for their wives having an affair. This is the essence of the double standard philosophy.

James was living the double standard to the hilt. But I was never sure of this. His love letter had given me new hope. I couldn't have imagined he was having two more affairs during his trip to South America. It's difficult to comprehend both his love letter and his affairs at the same time. One of the most amazing insights for me about this whole experience was coming to the realization that it's possible for anybody to think and act in such contradictory ways. All my efforts to figure out whether James was having affairs were based on assuming his actions made sense. But this kind of contradiction didn't make sense to me—so I had no chance of figuring things out. No wonder I was always so confused.

Since I tried to make things fit, I didn't suspect him during that trip after receiving the love letter. It was a good period for me. It was all the more pleasant because I spent a lot of that time preparing for a show we were putting on at the tennis club in May to open the new tennis season. I wrote some special words for a tennis song and also practiced an old favorite blues tune. I especially enjoyed working on a dance number to demonstrate current rock steps. This was my first opportunity to wear the silver dress James had given me for Christmas.

My spirits were high. It was great to be putting my energies into something like this. I even started thinking I might get back into doing some singing or dancing...but I felt more comfortable with the idea of doing some kind of office work. At least I was thinking of doing something on my own. I was finally gaining some self-confidence,

Things weren't completely calm, however. I faced a number of challenges that summer that tested my strength and sanity. First of all, James decided to invite Terry and a guy she knew to our house for brunch one Sunday. I had mixed feelings about it. On one hand it would be a terrible ordeal. But on the other, I tended to think maybe he wasn't having an affair with her if he felt comfortable about having her come to the house. I was very uneasy, but managed to get through it.

There were other social events that summer where I was thrown with Terry. Each time was difficult, but one time in particular was a very painful experience. Terry and I were changing clothes in the same room following a swimming party. Seeing her nude body and imagining James making love to her, I thought I was going to die.

It's OK to Have An Affair If...

On the fourth of July, James was invited to a party in a nearby town given by a man he had a number of business dealings with. Tony was a real entrepreneur—into all kinds of deals and projects. James was fascinated by him. He worked unpredictable hours and had no regard for normal sleeping habits. Several times he called at 4:00 in the morning just to discuss an idea he was excited about. And sometimes he and James would start with dinner and work right through the night.

The fourth of July party he was having was for "business," so wives weren't invited. I suspected Terry might be invited through business connections. I told James I didn't want him to go with her. I explained that it was hard for me to accept another woman going with him when I couldn't. I surprised myself at being that assertive, but it worked—in a sense. James didn't go with her. He drove alone to the party. But when he got sleepy driving home and almost ran off the road, he implied that my jealousy in asking him not to go with Terry had caused him to risk his life. I got the feeling that even when I won, I lost.

Tony was big on entertaining. James and I were invited to several parties he had with his wife. Often Terry was invited too. I felt a lot of pressure to look good in comparison to her or any other woman there. I felt successful when Tony said I was the sexiest-looking woman he'd ever seen. But I didn't feel sexy. I was working too hard at pretending to be self-assured.

I began doing everything possible to make James think I trusted him. I made a policy of never looking in his briefcase or his pocket calendar. Not only did I not look, I made sure he knew I was committed to giving him this privacy. I continued to think it was risky to let him see I didn't trust him. I certainly didn't want to be in the position of pushing him into something, just in case I was wrong.

BEYOND AFFAIRS

James:
I don't know what effect it would have had if Peggy had questioned me directly about her suspicions. As long as she was indirect, it was easy for me to be evasive. The last thing I ever wanted was to have an open discussion about affairs. If she had asked me point-blank, "Are you seeing another woman?", I feel sure it would have changed me in some way. There were times when I probably would have lied and said no. This was more true in the early years of my affairs when I didn't think Peggy had much reason to be suspicious and I thought I could bluff my way through a confrontation if it occurred. There were times later on when I thought she might know. I don't know that I could have lied then. I've never been a good liar. I'm sure I wouldn't have continued if she'd persisted in confronting me.

Peggy:
I was not ready for a confrontation. I still hoped I was wrong. I continued to act like I really trusted him. Another policy I adopted was never calling him when he was out of town. He hadn't told me not to call (in the way he'd told me not to call him at the office). But I didn't. If he were gone for a week, he usually called two or three times. On the nights when he called after dinner, I felt relieved, thinking he was safely in his hotel room. Little did I know there were actually times when he called me while another woman was waiting in the bathroom. On the nights he didn't call, I was much more restless and concerned. But worst of all was when he called in the daytime. I invariably thought he was calling then because he planned to be with a woman that night and wanted to make sure I wouldn't need to talk to him later.

I also didn't question him about his activities on his trips. I tried to satisfy my curiosity by getting him to talk about his trip without asking direct questions. I didn't want him to think I was suspicious, but I did want as much information as possible. Somehow, the more he talked, the better I felt.

It's OK to Have An Affair If...

James:

I continued to complicate my life. I was still seeing Lisa in New York, although not nearly as often as during the past two years. I'd stopped seeing Marge in Washington in the early fall, but I'd begun another relationship there soon after. During this same period I developed a close friendship with Martha, a grade school teacher who was part of a group I worked with one night a week for most of the school year. The group was composed of grade school teachers and their principal. The primary purpose was to examine their relationships at school and work on ways to improve their effectiveness. In actuality, we ended up focusing more on personal growth than team effectiveness. They were very eager for any kind of personal exploration. During our group sessions, several members were able to express feelings and deal with issues that had been buried in their guts for a long time.

Martha functioned as a co-trainer with me, so it was common for us to have planning meetings in addition to our group sessions. We also talked on the phone three or four times a week. She was good at keeping me informed about issues at school, and we enjoyed talking about other interests we had in common. We never got sexually involved, but in every other way I was probably as intimate and caring with her as I'd ever been with any woman.

I probably would have tried to have sex with her if she had not been married and I hadn't been involved with Terry. It just wasn't practical to start another relationship in the same town. Even I had enough brain left in my head to see that. Peggy and Terry were suspicious of my friendship with Martha and jealous of the time we spent together. Terry was more vocal of her jealousy than Peggy. With both of them, however, I felt justified in making light of their suspicions. After all, I was completely innocent of any misdeeds—as long as thoughts and plans didn't count.

My friendship with Martha was unique for me. I haven't been that close to another woman without sex or fears about sex getting in the way. We liked each other and were able to express our liking without adding the extra complications that come with sex. Martha was strong and soft. I valued our relationship at the time, but in retrospect I appreciate it even more. I wish I had more friends like her.

Peggy:
James' involvement in personal growth groups seemed to take him further away from me than anything had ever done before. I was especially upset because he got so close to the people in the groups and shared a lot of personal information. I was afraid he might share personal stuff about us that would embarrass me or put me in a bad light.

At the same time, there were some very positive changes in his personality as a result of his involvement in the groups. He learned to show his emotions more easily. While I would normally have been overjoyed at this, I couldn't bring myself to accept that these important changes were being caused by his relationship with people I didn't even know. I felt left out of his life and scared of what changes might be next.

I wasn't the only one having trouble with personal growth groups. The groups James ran with his class (mostly male) created problems for the wives of some of the students. So one of James' colleagues formed a group of spouses and a few other interested people. We met one night a week for about six weeks. What I experienced wasn't all that reassuring, but it wasn't as bad as I'd imagined. I felt better just knowing what it was like.

I still was concerned about the women in some of the groups. I especially didn't like it when they would go away overnight. The time I got most upset was when James organized a weekend for one group to go to a cabin of Tony's out in the country. My fears were even greater at the idea of going to this isolated cabin in the woods rather than a public meeting site. I felt this was just a way to arrange to have a good time while making it look like work. I admitted to being jealous and questioned his judgment in taking the group there.

He debated me down as usual with his superior posture of "You just don't understand—This is business—Your thinking is narrow—How can you question my judgment on how I handle my job?" I was miserable.

I think I was always intimidated by the fact that James had a Ph.D. and I had only two years of college. Also, I think the fact that his Ph.D. was in psychology made me think he knew more than me about almost everything. I had helped make him "god," set about worshipping him, and resented every minute of it.

It felt like we were on a course that could only lead to the end of our marriage if I didn't start speaking up about my feelings. I decided to try:

"I feel you're getting more and more committed to pursuing your interests and your career without considering the effect it's having on me or our relationship. I need to know where I stand."

He said, "I'm trying not to let the success of either area of my life be at the expense of the other."

I still didn't know where I stood with him, but I wasn't even clear about what I wanted any more. I wasn't sure I understood myself enough to have any chance of making him understand my feelings. I figured that writing it down might help me think more clearly. So I wrote the things I couldn't yet say to him, and kept them safely hidden.

I have an uneasy feeling that one clay I'll feel so unnecessary to your life and so much in the background that I'll owe it to myself to get out before I'm destroyed. I sometimes wonder if I could be any more unhappy without you than I am with you. My life is dominated by feelings of hurt rejection, insecurity, and frustration The only times I feel free to any degree are in situations completely separate from you or when you're gone on a long trip. That's the only time I'm sure of myself or really relaxed I don't know exactly why that is. Maybe it's the uncertainty of our activities together. I feel you're elusive—that I can never completely depend on you to do anything or be anywhere without a real possibility of being disappointed Also maybe it's because I feel so self-conscious around you. I'm concerned with your reaction to everything I say and do so I can never relax. I feel like I'm always being tested. I constantly try to act in such a way as to get your love and approval.

I desperately need to develop a better self-image. I've got to face the possibility of being on my own I've got to risk confronting you at least a little in order to have any chance of making things better. I can't go on indefinitely like this.

It was clear that I had to start telling him how I felt on an ongoing basis. This was the beginning of a period when we had some of our toughest conversations. I was more direct than I'd ever been about my feelings—especially about other women. When a woman was assigned to work with him on a project that included the possibility of their traveling together, I was scared to death...and I said so.

"I've done a lot of reading. I know work-related affairs are common. I also know travel makes them more likely. I don't want you to travel with Diane. It scares me to think about it. I couldn't stand it if you ever had an affair."

I was trying to tell him some of my feelings that I'd never been willing to admit before. It seemed safer to talk about this new situation than about my suspicions of an affair with Terry. My tactic didn't work. He became very self-righteous and defensive.

"I won't let you interfere with my work. I'm dedicated to doing a good job and won't put up with your petty jealousies."

James:
I wasn't involved with Diane at the time, but Peggy was right in sensing the possibility. I was very attracted to her

and decided in my own mind that if I ever broke up with Terry, she would be the next woman I would pursue. She was single and more available than Martha. I also picked up clear non-verbals from her that she was attracted to me. We worked together on several projects, becoming increasingly intimate without direct sexual involvement. I think we both knew it was just a matter of time.

Peggy:

Just as I thought there was no hope left, Terry quit and moved to another city. I felt tremendous relief. I even felt some compassion for her. I thought she might have been having some of the same problems I was having with James—like the amount of time he was spending with the personal growth groups and other activities. No matter why she was leaving, I saw it as a positive thing. Even though I thought I might never know the extent of their relationship, I was glad it was over.

James:

Several things came together to end my affair with Terry. We saw much less of each other during the summer, mainly because of my change in routine. During the school term it had been easy to see her several times a week. It was simply a matter of tacking a few more hours onto my normal routine. Not so in the summer. I wasn't teaching and had no need to keep regular office hours. I played a lot of tennis that summer at a club near my house which she couldn't be any part of. The net effect was a significant decrease in our involvement, both in terms of intensity and frequency. We never talked directly about it, but I think we were both aware it wasn't working.

Then came the fall and my working relationships with Martha and Diane. I think Terry accepted I wasn't sexually involved with either of them, but she resented the obvious closeness we had and the amount of time I spent working with them. The final blow came in October when my friend,

Frank, came to Rochester for a visit. I was busy at the time his flight arrived and asked Terry to pick him up at the airport. I told her about his prowess as a chaser and assured her he'd try to go to bed with her, but that I didn't want that to happen. All to no avail. They did go to bed. I knew I had no right to decide who Terry got involved with; but Frank was such a blatant chaser, I thought I had to protect her. I guess it was me I was protecting. I had trouble accepting it. Soon after that incident we agreed to stop seeing each other.

It was the toughest parting of all my affairs. We weren't fighting and there was no bitterness—just sadness and a reluctance to let go. She finally decided to leave the city. I think it was best for both of us that she did.

Peggy:
Another important event took place about this time. James made a major decision about a change in his career. After almost eight years of teaching—six years in Pittsburgh and almost two years in Rochester—he decided to stop teaching and go into full-time consulting. He'd been doing some part-time consulting for the past four or five years. He clearly preferred that work and decided to devote full time to it.

He had more connections in Pittsburgh, so we decided to move back at the end of the 1969-70 school term. The really important part of this decision as far as I was concerned was that he wanted me to work with him in a secretarial and administrative role—at least until he could get established and hire some other people.

James:
Before leaving Rochester I had one more in-town affair—with Diane. I entered this one very cautiously. I was still somewhat gun-shy from my deep involvement with Terry and the way it had ended. My caution didn't pose any problem for Diane. She wasn't looking for a heavy involvement. We had a lot of professional interests in

common, so we enjoyed spending time together. We also enjoyed having sex, but it never took on the central focus that it did in most of my other affairs.

I did have one unique sexual experience with Diane. Or maybe I should say non-sexual. One night I was unable to get an erection. It was the first and only time it ever happened to me. We were already nude and engaging in some casual foreplay. I felt excited and was interested in having intercourse. As it became clear I wasn't getting an erection, I got worried. I didn't say anything at first. I just kept trying. Finally, I became frustrated. I told Diane I couldn't get it up. I was embarrassed, but she handled it beautifully. She first tried a little direct assistance. That didn't help. She then suggested we just relax and enjoy ourselves—that it was nothing to be concerned about. I couldn't completely relax, but the fact she didn't see it as a problem kept me from getting a lot more preoccupied with it. She was right. The next time we were together, I got an erection as usual and never experienced any difficulty again. Needless to say, I was relieved. I also had a lot of respect for Diane's maturity in the way she dealt with the situation.

This affair lasted only four or five months and never reached the boiling point for either of us. Just a good, satisfying relationship. Knowing I was leaving town in the summer probably helped us keep the lid on. Our parting was easy and friendly.

Peggy:
I never strongly suspected this affair with Diane. I had a sense of false security since they never did travel together. I was so relieved at that—and at Terry's moving away—I was not as suspicious as in the past.

I still felt some of the old uncertainties, but not nearly so strong. The months passed swiftly as we made plans for the work we would do together. I think it was the anticipation of working with James that made me happy to be moving, even though this would be our fifth move in five years. Every time, I'd found some reason to be optimistic, thinking it would be positive for our relationship. This time I especially felt that way.

In the months before we moved James called on me a couple of times in a work-related capacity. Once he asked me to tape a reading for use in some of his workshops. Another time he asked me to typeset a training exercise when the secretaries didn't think they could do it in time. It meant renting a typewriter of a kind I'd never used before and typing all night—but I did it. He was very proud of me. More importantly, I was proud of myself.

Things were changing-slowly, but surely. The most distinct sign of the change came a couple of months before we moved when he actually began saying, "I love you." It had been four long years since I'd heard him say those words. I'd carefully saved the few letters where he'd written it—but it was wonderful to hear it again.

6

A Time of Transition

Peggy:

Our move back to Pittsburgh in June of 1970 was the beginning of a significant transition for our marriage and for me personally. I worked with James in setting up an office downtown—getting furniture, office equipment, and other basics. He hired another professional and a secretary, so there were four of us working that first summer. The original idea was for me to work only until he could hire enough people. He hired another secretary in September, and I stopped working.

For two months, in September and October, I was freer than I'd ever been in my life. Both kids were in school all day for the first time. Andy was in first grade and Vicki was in third. I played a lot of tennis. I also took a six-week intensive First Aid course—something I'd wanted to do for a long time.

BEYOND AFFAIRS

In November James hired another professional, and I went back to work to do typesetting...after taking a course to learn how to do it. I spent most of the next year typesetting brochures and training exercises. Several times when James was out of town I took both kids with me to the office at night. They thought this was great fun. I worked all night while they slept in the adjoining office. Sometimes I'd finish before daybreak and lie down beside them. We'd get up early, go home, and get ready for school. They loved this adventure and looked forward to telling the story to their friends.

I thoroughly enjoyed working and especially liked being involved with James. It felt good to recognize again after all these years that I was capable of contributing in this way. I'd wanted to be a full-time mother while the kids were preschoolers, but I'd had the distinct feeling this had contributed to the somewhat separate lives James and I had led since the kids were born.

James:
My involvement with Peggy was significantly different from the university years. A lot of changes had occurred which neither of us had planned or anticipated. When I left a very secure university job in June of 1970, it was for two primary reasons. I wanted to do more consulting, which I enjoyed, and I wanted to develop a consulting firm that would eventually allow me to make a lot of money. I hadn't thought through the lifestyle changes that would result from this move.

I'd had a lot of flexibility in my university job. I worked hard by my own choosing; but on the whole, it was not a very demanding job. I was in for a rude awakening. Developing a consulting firm required more time and energy than I ever imagined. The problem of obtaining working capital kept me occupied well into most nights during that first year. Financial backing I thought was firmly committed never came through. This had two important consequences. I was preoccupied with our financial survival to the point where I had little energy left for affairs, and I really needed Peggy's continuing contribution at work in order to make it.

Peggy:

I liked working with James. I was also involved with him and another couple in opening a gift shop. Between 1970 and 1971 we renovated an old brick building for the shop. We spent a lot of time attending to the many details required to get a small business in operation. It was very different from our earlier years in Pittsburgh. Then I'd been primarily a hostess. Our social life had been extremely active, but this time we rarely entertained. We were putting most of our energy into work.

One of the few parties we attended that first year was a New Year's Eve party. It led to a significant change in our lives—more specifically in our sex lives. We were talking to a group of people at the party when one couple began describing the difficulty they'd had in responding to their kids who had come home asking about "69." The group laughed about this and commented on the awkwardness of such a situation. Apparently they all knew what "69" meant—or were pretending, like I was. I looked at James and realized he didn't know what they were talking about either. We had never heard of "69." Not only did we not know it referred to mutual oral sex, but we didn't even know oral sex was an acceptable practice between men and women. We'd heard references to homosexuals who did such things, but had never guessed it was something we might include in our sex life.

We made it our business to find out about it and to try it. We were awkward at first. I didn't know just what to do, and neither did James. So I just started experimenting. It was easy to tell I was on the right track by his reaction. I must admit I had a lot more difficulty dealing with his efforts to please me. I couldn't relax. I was sure he didn't really want to do it. I thought I must smell bad—I must taste bad. All my conditioning had led me to think of my genitals as something you shouldn't put your hands on. The idea of putting your mouth on them was just about unthinkable.

Part of my misgivings were reinforced by James' natural caution in the beginning. Like me, he needed some time to get used to the idea, as well as the different taste and smell. I interpreted his caution as hesitancy and therefore didn't enjoy it as much as I did later on when we overcame our initial inhibitions. Now I find it one of the most pleasurable sensations in the world. I only wish we'd known about it sooner.

At first we did it only as a prelude to regular intercourse. It took several years for me to be comfortable with the idea of having him ejaculate in my mouth. Oral sex created a major change in our sex life—for the better.

James:
Some other key changes occurred during that first year out of the university setting. In developing a workshop in life-work planning, I began a reexamination of my own values and goals. That process is still going on, but I gained some useful clarity during that year. I learned I was in the right kind of work. Consulting in the development of human potential suits me. I love learning and being a part of other's learning. I found I did not enjoy managing others. Being responsible for me is enough.

I also learned that money didn't deserve the honored place I'd given it in the list of what's important in life. I'm still wrestling with just where it belongs in the spectrum of values, but I've definitely moved it down a few notches. It was logical to dissolve my consulting firm at the end of that first year. We weren't making it financially and I'd learned it wasn't the way I wanted to invest myself.

On the positive side, Peggy and I added some new dimensions to our relationship. It was a change in course we badly needed—from being on different roads going in the opposite directions to being on the same road traveling in

A Time of Transition

the same direction. On the negative side, I developed a severe case of workaholism. Despite the financial stress, I liked what I was doing. I got lots of goodies out of it. I didn't have to force myself to work late nights and Saturdays. It was easy to give up tennis and affairs. Not that I gave them up completely, but I cut back the time I spent in both areas by about ninety percent.

Peggy:

While James was working very hard, he wasn't traveling the way he'd done the past few years. There were still some occasions when he made short trips, usually just back to Rochester for a day or two.

On one of these trips I found my old fears returning. He'd planned to drive home on Sunday morning, and I started expecting him about noon. He didn't get home until 5:00 p.m. I knew he didn't have any business on Sunday, and I found it hard to believe he'd slept until noon. But I thought maybe I was just too suspicious. Things seemed to be so close between us and I knew so much about his activities—it seemed unlikely he would be involved with another woman. Anyway, I decided not to accuse him or make an issue of it. Things were going too well to blow it now.

James:

My first few trips back to Rochester had been strictly business. That didn't last long. Peggy's suspicions were well founded. I extended the weekend trip she described above to start an affair with Susan, a legal secretary in Rochester.

I'd met her about eight months earlier when I began a long series of negotiations in the office where she worked. I remember noticing she was attractive, but the negotiations were very important and I was focusing almost a hundred percent of my attention on them. On the day we finally reached an agreement, Susan was in and out of the conference room, typing up the contract as we drafted it. With the work done, I was able to relax and really look at her for the first time. I liked what I saw. She wasn't wearing a bra and she had a lovely figure. She noticed my excitement and a little electricity began to flow between us as we made eye contact. I was delighted to learn she was single and yes, she'd like to have dinner with me that night.

It was a nice evening but we didn't make it all the way. We danced in a way I thought would surely lead to bed, but at the eleventh hour, she said no. She was involved with another guy and didn't want to mess it up. I assured her I felt the same way about my relationship with Peggy, but she was unwilling to take the risk. I kept thinking she might change her mind at any minute. It was clear she wanted to make love as badly as I did. But she stood firm. I stayed over another night, feeling certain her resolve wouldn't hold up. But it did. I tried to accept it graciously, but I couldn't hide my disappointment. In parting I asked her to call me if she ever decided our relationship could go further.

About two weeks later I was surprised and extremely pleased when she called me at the office in Pittsburgh.

"I've changed my mind," she said. It was as simple as that.

"I'm glad," I replied. What an understatement! "When are you coming to Rochester again?" "Hold on a minute and I'll tell you." I glanced at my calendar and made a date on the spot.

"You realize the last two numbers in my phone number are 69, don't you?" "No, I hadn't noticed," I acknowledged, "but I like it." I could hardly believe my ears. Her playfulness reminded me of Lisa. Sweet anticipation! I don't know of anything that compared with the build-up of excitement that began with that conversation...and I had thought I was unlikely to hear from her again.

I managed to tie some business purpose into my trip to Rochester, but I don't remember what it was. What I do remember is having dinner with Susan, going back to her apartment and devouring each other. She was serious about oral sex. She liked it and was right up front about it. My experience with it was still quite limited. Peggy and I had started to experiment a little, but we were somewhat tentative. There was nothing tentative about Susan's approach. Her enthusiasm was catching. For the first time I began to really enjoy both sides of oral sex.

I saw Susan about once a month in Rochester until she moved to Kansas in the spring of 1972. Our relationship was based almost totally on our mutual enjoyment of sex. We enjoyed having a good dinner and some dancing as a warm-up, but sex was clearly the main event. And oral sex was always an integral part of it. Seeing each other so infrequently worked well for both of us. We lived in very different worlds and didn't have a lot to talk about. But for one night a month we really enjoyed ourselves. I saw Susan last in October, 1972, when I attended a conference in Kansas. It was a good night as usual—not passionate love, just good sex.

My experience with Susan made a positive contribution to my sex life with Peggy. I'm not about to make the next leap in the rationalization process and say it justified the affair. I'm just acknowledging that occasionally there are some benefits for the primary relationship. The positive oral sex I had with Susan helped me get beyond some of my initial inhibitions. I was then able to pursue it more enthusiastically with Peggy. On her part, Peggy didn't need any prodding. She was willing and eager to experiment and expand our lovemaking.

It still amazes me that we were so late in learning about such a basic sexual experience as oral sex. That's unlikely to happen anymore. There are too many books and magazines dealing with it explicitly for young people to miss knowing about it. Not so in our childhood years. If anyone was doing it in our hometown in Mississippi, it was a well-kept secret. It was strictly a taboo topic. Despite the general lifting of sexual inhibitions, it is still taboo for many. It took us about three years after the first time we tried it to overcome our inhibitions and queasy feelings about it. Now it's finally a natural and highly valued part of our sex life. Of all we've learned about sex, I think it has added more sheer pleasure and variety to our lovemaking than anything else. Like Peggy, I wish we'd discovered it earlier.

Some of you are thinking, "This is terrible. He shouldn't be having oral sex—much less talking openly about it." One reason for writing this book is our belief that we need more honest communication about sex. Sex is too important to expect each couple to "reinvent the wheel." I'm not saying everyone should engage in oral sex. It will always be up to each couple to experiment and decide for themselves what gives them pleasure. I am saying—let's share what we know from our own experience. Too many people feel trapped in boring sexual relationships because they don't know about some of the options that could enrich and bring some excitement into their sex life. And frequently they resist asking for help because it would imply they have failed. Since so few people talk openly about their sexual problems, it's easy to conclude you're the only one having any.

It's a terrible irony. If I discover a new way to cook a standing rib roast, I'll tell everyone at the cocktail party. But if I discover a new way to enjoy sex, I probably won't tell a soul. I may not even tell my partner! If I'm having trouble with my tennis swing, I'll discuss it with anyone who'll lend a sympathetic ear—especially if I think they know something about tennis. But if I'm having trouble with my sex life, chances are I won't mention it to anyone. We talk and share the most about the least important things in life, and least about the most important things.

We don't need to go to the other extreme. We don't all have to "go public" with our sex lives. What we need is enough appropriate disclosure so that we can learn from each other and gain the support from sharing that's available to us in almost every other area of our lives. Count yourself lucky right now if you have at least one other person you talk openly and freely with about your sexual experience. It doesn't count if you're paying them to listen or if they don't reciprocate.

Some of you may be feeling a lot of resistance to the idea of talking about such private matters. You learned, like I did, that it's not nice to talk about sex. Since we've had so little experience at it, many of us feel we simply can't do it. We'd be too embarrassed. We've also been taught it would violate the trust of our partners and diminish the experience. This may be true if we're living with the belief that all talk about sex is taboo. It is not true when we accept sex as a natural, important part of our lives and recognize that talking about it can build as well as destroy trust—enrich as well as diminish our experiences. Our attitudes, intentions, and the way we talk about it make all the difference. As a boy, the primary place I learned to talk about sex was in the locker room. Locker room sex talk does tend to violate trust and diminish one's experience. This is not what I'm recommending. I'm suggesting that there are appropriate times and places for talking intimately about your sex life with people you trust and care about. You don't even have to be skilled and experienced in the way you talk about it. As long as you are doing it out of caring for all concerned, it will likely have a positive effect.

I just became aware again of an amusing, but not insignificant, block to talking openly about sex. We seldom know the right words to use. Oh, we know the proper words, but they don't "feel" right—and neither do the slang terms we grew up with. I've been using the phrase "oral sex" partly as an easy way to refer to both major forms, but also because it seems like a fairly neutral phrase I'm comfortable with. To be more specific, I have a difficult time using "cunnilingus" to refer to the male act of placing his mouth on the female genitals. It's too formal for me. And it doesn't capture any of the essence of the activity. "Eating pussy" suits me a lot better, but I realize some of you just felt a pit in your stomach. It's so crude sounding. It just won't do in some company. Likewise, "fellatio" sounds like something that ought to happen in an opera, but "blow job" sounds demeaning. And "giving head" is not much better.

You may be saying, "This is awful! Why is he dwelling so much on those words?" My answer is twofold. First, the serious one. I'm tired of participating in the charade. I think most of us are unnecessarily constrained or inhibited by our lack of comfort in talking about sex—especially with members of the opposite sex. One of the secrets to getting what you want in life is to ask for it. But how can you ask for it if you're not comfortable with the words? I know—the romantic ideal is to have everything just happen, as if by magic. Let's face it. Things don't always just happen, but we can do something about it. Talking directly about sex can enhance our sexual activities considerably—during the act itself as well as in the arousal stage. We need to check out the particular words we use. The same word may arouse and excite one person and turn off another. It's also easy to be confused by different usages of the same word. I grew up thinking cock always referred to the female genitals, but I've since learned that most people use cock to refer to the penis.

The second part of my answer is, I think it's funny. If you can get beyond your own positive and negative loadings for certain words, I think you can appreciate the ridiculous way most of us have learned to talk about sex. Or perhaps I should say, the ways we've learned to talk around sex. Even the functions associated with our sexual organs get assigned cute names—I guess for the benefit of children. For many of us, these words we learn as children stick with us, so it's not unusual to hear a conversation like the following between two adults.

"Pull in at the next service station, dear. I need to tinkle." "OK, I need to do 'number 2' myself."

Check out the words you use with your love partner. How do you refer to some of the basics, like *intercourse* and *orgasm*? What are your favorite words for the male and female genitals? Are you comfortable using these with your partner, or do you use them only in thought? Are there any words you can't use? Why? I guarantee, you'll be amazed and amused at what you discover.

Peggy:

Most words about sex were taboo when I was growing up. I got the feeling that I shouldn't even think about sex, much less talk about it. I think this idea of "sex is bad" has had a big impact on the lack of "good" words related to sex. I've had a hard time trying to develop a sexual vocabulary. I've never been satisfied with the technical names for my sexual anatomy, but all the slang terms have negative connotations because of their use in jokes that are derogatory to women. I have some of the same problems with words describing the male genitals. "Down there" is hardly a good description of a person's genitals, either male or female, but it's typical of the kind of words we resort to in trying to talk about sex. It seems to me that we are in need of a whole new sexual vocabulary, without all the vague or negative overtones, in order to really communicate about this important area of our lives.

Most of our communication during this period, however, was focused on other things. In August of 1971 James decided to give up the idea of developing a consulting firm and continue full-time consulting on his own. I handled his secretarial work from the office of the gift shop—which we opened in October of 1971. I did the bookkeeping, handled the correspondence, and filled orders for training materials. I also read as much as possible about training and management development in order to broaden my own understanding.

James:

I threw myself into developing our gift shop and consulting out of our basement office. Peggy was intimately involved in both activities. Some couples can't bear to think of working together. Living together is problem enough. At this time in our lives it was therapeutic for us. We grew closer and carried on a continuing dialogue about what we wanted out of life. This was quite a contrast to the separation we had developed when I was working at the university and she was a housewife.

Peggy:
This was a time of growing confidence for me. Besides the work I was doing with James and the work in the shop, I still took time to be involved with activities related to the kids. I saw myself as almost totally responsible for their care. At the time I accepted it as natural that I should do so much outside work and all the work at home. One benefit of this was that I became very well organized. I had to be. I arranged for a babysitter after school the three days a week I worked late. Sometimes the kids came by after school. Things were really fast-paced...but I was thriving on it.

I loved the environment of the shop. We sold both manufactured and hand-crafted items. The "artistic" atmosphere led me to decide to wear long skirts all the time. I also let my hair grow long. When I was twenty-five I'd thought I would never again be able to wear my hair long—that I'd be too old. But at thirty-five I felt younger than ever. I also began to go without a bra occasionally. I really liked the natural feeling of this way of dressing. It had nothing to do with the "burn-the bra" movement. It related to my feeling more relaxed and comfortable with myself. As my life continued to change in that direction, so did my attitude about dress, so that within a couple of years I stopped wearing a bra completely.

I had also been changing my attitude toward James. For my birthday in February of 1972, he gave me a beautiful ring. Symbolically, this was important. I hadn't worn my wedding ring since 1968 when I'd removed it in silent protest. We had developed a close friendship with a talented goldsmith whose work we sold in our shop. James knew how much I loved her rings and asked me to choose one. I chose a raised petal shape that she called a lacybloom. She

A Time of Transition

placed the diamond from my engagement ring in the middle and called it a dewdrop. With the ring, James gave me a card which said, "Life is beautiful with you."

A few months later, on our anniversary in May, I surprised him with a ring our friend made called a "king ring—for a king of a man." This reflected the positive feelings I was developing toward him. Things were slowly turning around. We started talking in ways we hadn't talked before—about our hopes and fears and goals for our life together.

In the summer of 1972 we held a life/work planning session at our house for a group of about twelve people, most of whom were friends and/or people James worked with in some way. James and I participated in this session personally and developed some specific plans. We decided to move back to the South, We hadn't intended to live in the North so long, but for ten years we'd done whatever we needed to do regarding job opportunities. Now we were being deliberate in choosing where and how we wanted to live.

Later that summer we made a trip down the east coast with the kids, specifically looking for a place we'd like to move. We thought we'd like Florida because we'd spent short periods there in the past and liked it. Before we left on our trip, however, some friends told us about Hilton Head Island, South Carolina. They thought it was a beautiful spot and recommended we stop off there on our way down.

We did stop by Hilton Head and found it delightful. It had lots of unspoiled natural beauty and the kids loved the beach. James and I had some of our most fun-filled times there on that trip—specifically at the beach. We went in the ocean with the kids, who were eight and ten at the time. We had them stay in close to shore while we went out a little farther, but still shallow enough to stand. James supported me in the water while I slipped off my bathing suit bottoms, and we had intercourse there in the ocean. It was a fun way to take care of a practical problem. A two-week trip with young children, sleeping in the same motel room, certainly cramps your style for lovemaking.

We checked out locations in Florida, as well as taking the kids to Disney World, but we didn't find just what we were looking for. We'd only spent one night at Hilton Head on our way down and had scheduled only one night on the way back to Pittsburgh. On that second stop we stayed almost all the following day and talked to real estate people. We'd been thinking of Hilton Head only as a resort location, but we began to realize there was a regular family community there too. And it seemed to offer a lot of things we were looking for in a simple lifestyle for us and the kids. James stopped off there several times that fall on business trips he made to Florida. Then in January, 1973, both of us went to Hilton Head and made a firm decision to move there that summer.

Lots of people thought we were crazy to move and give up the things we'd worked for in Pittsburgh. There certainly was a professional risk in making the move. But for me there was no question. I saw this as part of my long-range hope for really getting our lives together. It would mean leaving behind lots of people, places, and memories that had been painful for me. It meant a fresh start. I felt that maybe we had a chance to put the past behind us. James' attitude as represented by wanting to make the move seemed like a positive sign to me.

James:

The decision to move to Hilton Head was a good one for us. It was probably the first significant decision we ever made together after a careful examination of our options and what we wanted, individually and as a couple. There was clear financial risk, but overall it felt right to both of us.

Ironically, I started seeing Terry again during this period. It's not something I'd planned. I hadn't had any contact with her since she left Rochester in 1969. In

A Time of Transition

February, 1973, I began doing some management workshops in the city where she lived, and I was very curious about how her life was going. I called her for dinner one night and she accepted. Apparently she was curious about me too. We were as nervous as two kids on their first date. It didn't take long to see that our sexual attraction was still there. About ten seconds, in fact. Our first kiss hello told it all. The hurt from our parting was gone, or at least diminished enough not to interfere. I don't remember whether we went directly to bed or ate first, but it was a pleasant reunion. We saw each other about seven or eight times between then and September. The sex was good and it was fun to be with her, but there wasn't the kind of intense involvement we had the first time around. I think we both put limits on it, knowing it wasn't in either of our best interests to try to recreate that.

Peggy:

In February of 1973 James gave me a long black dress for my birthday. I wore it to a party that night, and I felt pretty for the first time in a long while. This was no doubt due to my feeling better about my relationship with James, as well as anticipating our move to Hilton Head. Little did I know that the very next week he would rekindle his affair with Terry. The irony of that timing is somewhat overwhelming. I didn't suspect anything—at least not at that point. There had been times in the past when I'd been concerned that he might see her again, but not after such a long time.

It was a terrible feeling later on to go back and compare the situation as I saw it during this period with the actual events that were taking place in James' life. In April, when the kids and I met James at Hilton Head to look at our house—he had just been with Terry. When he was away for a week in May and I was concentrating on organizing our office for the move—he was with her again. And in June when we attended a going away party held for us on the night James got back from a trip—he had just been with her.

BEYOND AFFAIRS

After we moved to Hilton Head, he saw Terry on most of the trips he made that summer. While I never consciously suspected anything, I was growing more and more frustrated and upset in general. I attributed it to the dilemma I was in, trying to entertain the kids while setting up our office at home. It was tough on the kids being in a new place and not knowing other children their age. Things just didn't seem to be working out the way I'd expected. I thought I should feel good, but instead I still felt uneasy and unhappy.

Things began to change in September when the kids started to school. I got involved with some new activities too, including leading Vicki's Girl Scout troop. The office work was much easier with the kids in school and more time to devote to it. I also got involved with the new racquet club. I served as a hostess for the first major tennis event there in September. I began to feel much better about things. I even felt sorry for James that he was away and missed this big tournament. Ironically, this turned out to be the last trip where he saw Terry. In retrospect, I think my improved feelings had more to do with some changes in his attitude toward me than with the physical circumstances of my life at that time.

A dramatic sign of his changing attitude was his asking me to join him at a conference in Chicago the following month. He had been attending these meetings for several years. After all my worrying about what he was doing at various conferences, he was actually suggesting I go with him to one.

We arrived in Chicago the day before the conference was to begin. That night we got into a big argument. I was irritated that he took no responsibility for either calling the kids or talking to them when I called. I figured we were both responsible for contact with the kids, but he was accustomed to leaving it up to me.

With that kind of beginning to the trip, I was concerned as to how the conference would go. One reason James had wanted me to come was to attend a pre-conference

A Time of Transition

workshop with him entitled "The Consultant and Significant Other." Obviously, I was the "significant other." We attended that session the next day—and it was a marvelous experience for us. It brought some clarity to the way we related, as well as the way we worked together.

The entire conference was a great success and gave me a chance to see how others reacted to me in this kind of setting. I knew I was doing a good job, and felt I was capable of doing more. This was confirmed by my experience at the conference.

Another important thing we did in Chicago was to purchase a book about couple relationships that covered all kinds of problems in marriage, including one chapter on affairs. I was very aware of the potential in making that purchase. It seemed to be one more step in moving us closer to honest communication. I knew the next step was to clear up the past, but I wasn't ready to tackle that quite yet. I wanted to enjoy this new stage of our relationship for awhile.

James:

The Chicago conference was definitely a significant event for us. I had been worried on the front side that it might not turn out well. Many of the guys at the conference were sure to be openly chasing women as usual. I felt a little like I was violating the unwritten code I had always bought into: "Don't bring your wife to the conferences. Even if you don't chase women yourself, it cramps the style of those who do." A lot of the men Peggy would be meeting knew I was a chaser. I thought most of them would be discreet enough to protect me, but I couldn't be sure. I was relieved to get through the conference without an incident.

The best part of the conference was the tremendous boost Peggy got in self-esteem. She was amazed at how much she knew about organizational development and how easy it was for her to relate to the workshops and papers being presented. It was also clear that people liked to talk with her. I don't think she was prepared for the acceptance she found. All of this had a visible effect on Peggy. She was a happier, more confident person.

I think the conference was just as important for me, but in a different way. For Peggy it signaled a beginning—for me, an ending. I had viewed conferences as my territory, a place for me to work and play apart from her. Starting my first affair at a conference probably added a symbolic element that I hadn't consciously thought about. Inviting her into my playground was the final stroke that ended the sharp role distinctions we had held since I started teaching in 1962. It was a clear signal that affairs had diminished in importance and my involvement with Peggy had taken on a new importance. I'm putting this understanding together in retrospect. It's not something I had sorted through at the time. In my mind I still placed a high value on chasing women, but in reality, I wasn't putting much energy into it.

Peggy:
For the next few months we were like newlyweds. Whenever he traveled I sent him love notes. He brought me back presents. Each of us seemed to be seeing each other through fresh eyes after years of confusion. James had written a long poem on trust that was published with a dedication to me. I wrote music to his poem that just flowed out of me with very little effort. I wrote poetry myself that flowed as fast as I could write it down. It was as if a dam had burst and the trapped energy was flooding out all at once.

At Christmas James gave me a "marriage contract" which he had altered to represent our particular situation—eighteen and a half years. It professed love and caring in a special way. I basked in it, confident it was true.

Our sex life reflected this new relationship. I felt relaxed and unpressured to compete or perform for the first time in years. I recall quite clearly the dramatic difference in the way I felt while making love the night before I was to leave

A Time of Transition

on a trip as opposed to the fear I'd felt all those years when he was about to leave. Our lovemaking was spontaneous and fun, with a lot of caring that was more than just sex.

In January, 1974, I made a trip to Richmond, Virginia, to attend a workshop on communication using TA (Transactional Analysis). The workshop was very positive for me, but the important thing was the trip itself. I had NEVER made a trip alone in my whole life. I was so excited I couldn't sleep at all the first night in the hotel. I wasn't nervous or upset, just wonderfully happy to be doing something completely on my own. The workshop only lasted a couple of days, but it was a big step for me. I realized what a "Child" I had been in my relationship with James and how it was possible to relate to him more as an "Adult." This meant not being controlled by my emotions.

But the immediate emotion was still excitement over my trip. I had flown to Richmond but took the overnight train to Savannah coming home. Once again, I lost a night's sleep. I was so excited on the train (as well as being afraid I wouldn't wake up for my stop at 7:00 a.m. the next morning) that I couldn't sleep. James met me at the train, but we only had time for breakfast together before he was to leave for a short trip. I talked as fast as I could to share as much as possible with him in the couple of hours we had together. I took him to the airport and then drove home to Hilton Head.

During the couple of days he was gone I kept thinking how much things had changed and wondering where all this would lead us. We were in a whole new ballgame, and I felt ready for whatever was to come. I didn't have long to wait.

7

Facing The Truth

James:

As I look back on it, I think the decision to tell Peggy about my affairs was inevitable. The double standard had been easy to maintain in the university years when our lives had been quite separate. But things had changed substantially. Our relationship had taken on a new meaning as we were moving out of the old role definitions of man and wife and taking our first tentative steps at forming a true partnership of equals. In the past year we'd started to focus more directly on improving our relationship than we'd ever done in the past. As we did this, I became more and more uncomfortable with the feeling she was playing with some cards missing while I had a full deck.

In spite of the missing cards, Peggy had grown tremendously in the last four years. She had a new sense of her worth as an individual. I knew in my gut she deserved more and would eventually demand more than the deceit I was giving her. In essence she was demanding more with her behavior, even though she never said it directly in words. J had a growing desire to be fair with her. I wanted to build our relationship and get it on a more equal footing. "Dealing" her the missing cards was a step in the right direction.

At the same time, I was struggling to clean up my own act, independent of Peggy. I wanted to be more authentic as a person and as a consultant. In my consulting work, I was preaching the value of honesty and openness while acting deceitfully in my most important relationship. At some point in every group I worked with, I would talk about the importance of being open and honest in developing trust in relationships. I'd explain away my deceit about affairs by saying there are probably a few things in every relationship that are best kept hidden—and affairs are one of them. This had worked for me for a long time, but in light of the energy Peggy and I were both investing in our relationship, it started to sound hollow.

I could write a formula now describing the likelihood of one or both partners in a relationship having affairs in the double standard as a function of their role distinctions and degree of involvement. I won't put it in mathematical form, but it goes like this: the sharper the role distinctions and the less the involvement, the greater the likelihood of affairs. As role distinctions are broken down and involvement increases, affairs are less likely. The pendulum was swinging for us. We had moved apart for a long time; now we were coming back together.

I think the crowning blow was our reading Loving Free, the book we bought in Chicago. We both liked the book. It was a candid description of how a couple worked through a lot of their sexual hang ups and developed a solid relationship through honest, deep communication. Peggy suggested we discuss the book, chapter by chapter. I agreed to this without really thinking it through. Once I did focus on it I didn't

Facing The Truth

know how I would handle the chapter on affairs. I'd never lied directly to Peggy and I didn't think I could. I know how crazy this sounds. I'd lied many times by inference and omission; but in my rationalizations, these didn't count.

All these things were operating in me, but not on a conscious level. I still thought I wanted to continue having affairs, and that I had to keep them hidden. I was shocked then, when I woke up at 3:00 a.m. in a New Jersey motel room and started thinking about telling Peggy. I was there on a two-day consulting job. I had not been with a woman. I hadn't tried. I just remember my surprise at waking in the middle of the night and thinking, "Now is the time for me to tell Peggy." To the best of my knowledge I'd never seriously entertained that thought before. I'd had countless discussions about affairs with other men on a continuing basis, but we never talked about the possibility of being honest with our wives. They invariably ended with something like, "It's a shame we can't tell our wives about this so they can enjoy it too, but that's impossible." "Yeh, you got that right."

I lay awake for four hours, thinking about it. I saw clearly for the first time that my relationship with Peggy couldn't grow any more until I told her. It was just too significant a thing to hide. I couldn't go on with the pretense of being a loving, committed husband...while doing something I knew she would be terribly upset about. My mind raced from one thought to another. We had a good thing going. I wanted to make it better—not break it up. How would she take it? Affairs had been a very positive, exciting part of my life. I didn't want to give them up. Could I cope with Peggy having affairs? Would she?

I knew I couldn't possibly predict her reaction. And I had the growing realization that I was going to tell her—I had to take the risk. I was scared shitless. I still remember the weird, unreal feeling I had as I finished my consulting job that morning and had lunch with my client, who was a personal friend and knew about my chasing around.

BEYOND AFFAIRS

"Ray, I'm going home tonight and tell Peggy about my affairs. " "Are you crazy? Don't do it. It'll break up your marriage. " "It might, but I don't think so."

I wasn't surprised at Ray's reaction. It's the same one I'd have had in any such conversation in the past. But it didn't change my mind. On the plane home that afternoon, I made some notes to organize what I wanted to say. I thought the way I got into it would be important and I didn't trust myself to freewheel it. I ate the steak dinner that night without really tasting it. Finally, I began.

"Are you up to some serious talk?" "Sure," Peggy quickly responded.

"I don't think you're going to like what I have to say," I cautioned. Her response had been too quick, too cheerful. I felt the need to prepare her a little for what was to come.

Peggy:

It's strange how I reacted to those words. Something inside me said, "This is it." I was surprised to realize I wasn't afraid. I felt a great relief at knowing it was all going to come out. We got the kids in bed, went into the bedroom, and undressed. We frequently talked in bed with the lights out, but James had some notes he wanted to use, so we sat nude on the bed facing each other with the lights on. I was as ready to hear as I could ever be.

James:

It felt ridiculous to be using notes as if I were making a presentation, but I needed them. I held both her hands, as much for me as for her. I felt unreal and needed the contact. Here's a copy of my notes which I followed closely:
"I want you to listen with understanding—with a lot of 'Adult' in TA terms.

You could help by telling me what I'm going to say, but don't. I need to say it.

It may sound melodramatic. I'm sorry about that.

Facing The Truth

I'm more scared than I've ever been about losing something special.

I'm taking the risk because I want to make it better.

I think we've both grown—the quality of our relationship is better than anything I ever imagined

I value you and love you more than I ever have before.

As I've felt you committing more and risking more in our relationship, it has become increasingly uncomfortable for me to keep some things hidden from you.

This is going to hurt both of us to some degree but I hope we can grow from it.

I am not involved with another woman now, but I have been in the past. (God it was hard to get that out.) I've always felt this was something we couldn't deal with, but I had no way of knowing how much we would change.

I decided early this morning that I couldn't be dishonest with you in discussing Loving Free.

I didn't feel guilty at the time I was with other women, but I've been feeling that way lately about hiding it from you.

With your growing interest in training and consulting, I can imagine us doing couples workshops together. There's no way I could do them without being open with you.

Maybe writing my piece on trust did it. I wanted to photograph you for the book, but it would have been too inconsistent.

In trying to understand and develop our relationship, this was too big a piece of reality to ignore or tiptoe around."

Peggy listened intently. I felt some relief and encouragement that she didn't react with an emotional outburst and she didn't pull away from me as I talked. I needed the supportive listening she was giving me. I'd made a start, but there was a lot more to come.

BEYOND AFFAIRS

Peggy:

I actually heard very little of what James said before he got to the point of, "Yes, he had been having affairs all those years." Finally—I knew for sure! But I wanted to know more. I'd lived with so many questions for such a long time. Now I wanted to check out all my suspicions and find out just who and where and when it all happened. He tried to tell me everything I wanted to know. I was pretty overwhelmed, but was hearing it the way he was telling it—with a lot of love and caring for me. To my surprise, and his, I continued to listen. I didn't cry or scream, or hit him, or any of the things he was afraid I might do. I believe my experience at the TA seminar earlier that week was a big help in being able to stay in my "Adult" through the whole thing and keep my emotions under control. My reaction was also affected by the tremendous relief I felt at finally knowing the truth.

James:

I hadn't planned to tell Peggy about the details of my affairs. In fact, I hadn't planned anything beyond telling her in general. When she asked for specifics, I gave them freely, letting her questions be the guide to how much. To my surprise, she wanted to know a lot, including specific things about the sex I had with some of my other partners. I'd started to relax a little, but now I felt renewed fear. I'd been encouraged by her initial acceptance of what I was telling her, but I didn't see how she could possibly listen to detailed descriptions without getting upset. I couldn't see any reasonable place to draw the line, so I answered all her questions honestly. I don't think I could have gone that far if she hadn't supported my disclosure in the way she did. Her eyes were bright with interest and we continued to hold hands or have some kind of physical contact the entire time. She expressed amazement, but not horror or shock. Her overwhelming reaction at this point was one of relief that it was finally out in the open. Her need to know was finally being satisfied.

Facing The Truth

Peggy:
I was relieved that the deceit was over and that he was being so totally open and honest with me. I think my reaction was largely determined by the reason for his honesty. If he'd been telling me just to unload or get it off his chest, it could have been unbearable. But it was clear he was doing it because he wanted to make things better. He was making an effort to ease the strain that had developed between us through so much dishonesty.

I was in control of my emotions while James was telling me. But later that night, when it really sank in, I felt sick at my stomach. Learning so much so quickly gave me the feeling of being on a roller coaster and not knowing how to get off. I felt like I might be dreaming.

I'm sure it would have been even worse if it had been completely unexpected. But I'd already suffered for years with my suspicions. This was a chance to check out the source of a lot of that pain. I also saw it as a chance to clear out the past, but that turned out to be much more difficult than I thought. I was surprised to learn he had continued to have affairs during the past few years when I'd felt sure nothing like that was going on. But the biggest surprise of all was that he still didn't want to give it up.

James:
Peggy was so absorbed in getting details about the past that what I said about the future didn't really register on her at first. I suppose there was also the strong cultural expectation operating that if a love partner ever makes a confession like I did, it ought to conclude with, "I'm sorry and I promise never to do it again." I was careful not to say that because it wasn't the way I felt. I did say I was sorry I'd done it in a deceitful way that had caused her pain. I didn't say I regretted doing it. On the contrary, I told her how much I valued the experiences—so much so, that I wanted both of us to be free to have affairs in the future. I wanted it all—a good thing with Peggy and affairs too.

BEYOND AFFAIRS

When she finally focused on this, she was visibly taken aback. Her first reaction was that she had no interest in having affairs. She couldn't even imagine herself doing it. It was clear this was an issue we weren't going to resolve quickly. I was so encouraged by the fact that we were talking productively about the whole thing, I quickly volunteered not to have any more affairs until we had talked it through and reached agreement on what we both wanted.

Peggy:
His attitude about both of us having affairs was a real shock. There were other surprises too. I'd assumed he felt guilty—but he'd rationalized all his actions as having nothing to do with me. I'd believed I could have some control over whether or not he had affairs by my own behavior—but he said nothing I did made any difference. I'd believed he wouldn't be involved in casual sex—that he would have to really care about someone—but his wide range of experiences included several very basic sexual encounters.

I felt a growing shyness with the realization that he had been intimate with so many other women. I began to feel awkward and self-conscious about my body. I wondered how the other women looked and how I compared. I realized all of them were much younger than me, and only one of them had ever had a child. This seemed like pretty stiff competition, even though I was in good shape. James had always been clear on how much he appreciated my body. He tried to reassure me by saying other bodies were just different, not necessarily better or worse.

We had started talking about 9:30 p.m. We finally quit at 2:00 a.m. Much to my surprise, we made love. I would have expected it to take quite awhile for me to feel loving toward him. I think I was feeling somewhat euphoric at finally knowing everything after so many years of uncertainty. But I soon came down to earth.

Facing The Truth

After James went to sleep, I lay awake trying to make sense of everything. My head was spinning. I spent the whole night thinking and writing. Here's some of what I wrote:

How could James not feel guilty Surely he had to Know he was hurting me. ~ can't imagine how anyone could do the things he did without feeling guilty. Doesn't he have a conscience. I can hardly believe he's the man I've been married to all these years. He seems like a total stranger. I need to remember he's the same person now as he was before he told me all this—only my Knowledge about him has changed

How could he still have been having affairs during the last few years We've been so involved with each other. I can't believe I was so fooled. I thought it was all in the past—not something to have to deal with now.

How can he still think it's possible to have affairs I'll never go back to the double standard. But I don't see any way I can have an affair. I can't imagine who or how or where. I don't even want to think about it. I need to talk an awful lot about this to get it clear in my head. How can he say his affairs had nothing to do with our relationship He says it wasn't personal—that it had nothing to do with me. Well, in my eyes it had everything to do with me.

And how can he say it didn't mean he was dissatisfied with me or our marriage He says nothing I could have done would have made any difference. He had completely separated his affairs from his life with me.

How could he separate the pain I was feeling from his actions—as if he had nothing to do with it He doesn't really understand my pain. He doesn't even see it. He wants us to put all this behind us and look to the future. But the pain won't go away that easily. It will take a lot of work.

I do think our relationship is more important to James now than it's ever been before. And I feel good about the sense of fairness he's shown by telling me the truth. A t last

BEYOND AFFAIRS

I'm being treated more like an equal. I'd always felt somehow less than him. But now that I don't feel guilty about having been jealous and suspicious, I feel much better about myself: I need that. I've got to depend on myself first now because I've got to be strong in dealing with all this confusion.

How can I ever deal with my pride? How can I face the people who knew all along? How can I keep other people from finding out. I don't think I can. I've got to find a way to hold up my head and see this through

I must remember my worth as a person is determined by me—by what I do—not by what James does. I need to deal with the hurt I feel at facing the facts. One way I can do that is to realize it's not as bad as the anxiety and pain I felt for so many years when I didn't know the facts.

I was able to make it through those years of doubt. Now I've got a chance to deal with it and make things better. I can't give up now. I've come too far.

The next day I felt better, like a big load had been lifted. I'd lived under a shadow of uncertainty for a long time. This was the beginning of a new way of looking at our relationship and at the world in general, There was even a kind of lightness to my feelings—maybe from exhaustion.

James awoke about 7:00 a.m. and we stayed in bed until after noon, talking constantly. This was really unusual for us, In the past, our pattern would have been to set it aside and go ahead with our usual responsibilities as if everything were normal. Vicki got off to school early and Andy was still home from school with a cold that had lasted several days. It's especially amazing I took this time for myself with a sick child at home. I was finally getting a sense of the importance of not always putting my needs last, I'd done that for too long.

By late afternoon I was feeling terrific. It's hard to explain how that could happen. Somehow I felt like I had a new lease on life. James and I took a walk on the beach, although this was only the first day of February. There was a growing openness to our feelings with each other—feelings of a deeper level of honesty than we'd ever had. Contrary to my expectations about being shy about sex for awhile, I found I was very turned on, and we had some terrific sex. This was the beginning of a renewed excitement with each other that seems to come with openness and honesty.

James:
It felt funny to be experiencing this new level of intimacy and at the same time have so many unresolved questions in our relationship. We were both amazed at this turn of events. I'd feared it might take months to build up any level of trust again, if it were possible at all. What I wasn't aware of was how low her trust level had been for years. So my telling her what she already suspected gave my credibility a big boost. She believed, and I agree, that the other significant factor in our building trust rapidly was my willingness to tell her everything she wanted to know.

Some people handle the issue of affairs by maintaining they don't want to know if their love partner has one. Some carry this approach even further and say they don't want to know the details, even after finding out their partner has been involved in an affair. Peggy was never close to being in either of these camps. It's fairly clear if I had refused to tell her the details she wanted to know, we could never have gone beyond that first revelation. It would have created some questions that could have hung between us forever. At the time I was telling her, I didn't appreciate the significance of this. I'm glad my spontaneous response to her questions was to go ahead and tell it all. Most men believe the opposite—that you should never disclose you had an affair...but if you're discovered and forced to acknowledge it, tell her as little as possible. It's a variation on the "what she doesn't know can't hurt her" routine. The rationale seems to be: "It's past. There's nothing we can do about it. Knowing details will only make it worse."

BEYOND AFFAIRS

Peggy:

This old "out of sight, out of mind" philosophy doesn't work. It's never out of mind. There's too much that you just can't understand or come to grips with if he's unwilling to discuss it. If you never get a chance to get any answers to your questions, they just fester and continue to be a barrier between you. Eventually, they are likely to kill the relationship—if not outwardly, at least in spirit. You may stay together, but "things will never be the same again."

Not all men are capable of discussing it to your satisfaction. They probably don't understand it themselves. Others who may be able to discuss it just aren't willing to put in the time and energy necessary to help you deal with it. And it does take some communication skills to have a fruitful discussion about such an emotional issue, especially with the person you feel is to blame for your hurt.

I do think it's important to be able to talk freely about your questions and your feelings in order to get beyond the pain and confusion. If this can't be done with your partner, there are plenty of other women who have "been there" and need the same kind of opportunity to talk candidly about their experiences. Women who find themselves in this situation could get together and work on helping each other. Not to bitch or gripe or moralize about how awful it is—but to talk honestly about how to understand their experiences and how to cope with them.

In the last chapter, I suggest some guidelines for talking through these issues in support groups. There's strength in knowing "you're not alone."

James:

There were some other surprises associated with my disclosure about affairs. I had learned to "manage" that part of my life reasonably well. Many people, including mutual acquaintances of Peggy's and mine, knew of my affairs. So far as I know none of them ever used that knowledge against me in a hurtful way. Over the years I'd learned to separate the affairs from the mainstream of my life, and I thought I was able to do this rather skillfully—without the use of a lot of energy. I was wrong.

Once I disclosed my affairs to Peggy, I immediately felt a sense of relief and a renewed energy for life. This really shocked me. I'd actually been using a lot of energy to keep all that stuff in place, but I hadn't been able to admit that to myself. I can see now this was all part of the rather elaborate rationalization process that allowed me to continue feeling OK about myself. Admitting how much energy it took to maintain the charade would have opened the door to feeling it was wrong.

I was also pleased to discover that cleaning up this area of my life had such a positive effect on my other relationships. Being at peace with myself allowed me to relate more easily to others. The risk of disclosure in all my relationships seemed much less. I'd taken the biggest risk I thought possible and the outcome was positive. As I see it in perspective, opening up to Peggy was far and away the most significant decision I've made in my life. It helped me get in touch with some basics about honesty.

Few people realize the positive power of appropriate honesty. Most of us heard some version of the platitude, "honesty is the best policy," while growing up, but we received a lot more direct training in how to be dishonest. And we were frequently punished for being honest, even though the implication beforehand was...if we would just be honest, everything would be OK.

Training in dishonesty takes many forms. Some of it seems very innocuous, especially when considered alone. In order to appreciate the significance of this early training, we need to consider that we are dealing with experiences that are cumulative in effect.

"Don't hurt other people's feelings" may be an admirable goal, but to an eight-year-old it means: "Be dishonest—pretend; don't let them know your true feelings; make up a feeling they'll like." "Wipe that frown off your face" may produce a more pleasing expression, but again, to an eight-year-old it means: "Be dishonest—don't show your true feelings in your facial expressions; it makes others (grown-ups) uncomfortable." So we learn to hide our true feelings by pasting on a smile or a blank expression.

We're also trained to assist others in their dishonesty. "Tell her I'm not at home—that I've gone shopping." Well intentioned parents train their children to be dishonest with these and other direct instructions. And we model dishonesty for our children. They see us hiding our true feelings and making up more acceptable ones. They see the little white lies and sometimes the large black ones. It's no wonder we're all fairly accomplished liars by the time we reach adulthood. And yet there seems to be in each of us a lasting desire to hear and tell the truth.

Of all the gifts any human being can give to another, perhaps the greatest is honesty. Love is good, but unless it's coming out of honesty, we can't really accept it and be nourished by it. In a sense honesty is love. It's like saying, "I love you and myself enough to take the risk of dealing with whatever is between us."

Life is simpler when we're honest. Perhaps this is one of the reasons we long for it. We've all known the beauty of this simplifying aspect of honesty, because we all begin life this way. Every small child is completely honest in their expressions until they're taught to be dishonest. Watch two-year olds. They move easily through the day, expressing likes and dislikes, joy and sorrow, pleasure and anger—with no pretense, no inclination of being anything but honest.

We talk about two-year-olds as having "boundless" energy. There's truth in that statement that goes beyond their seemingly endless activity during that stage of life. They're not concerned with questions of how to act. They do whatever they feel like. All their energy is available for living instead of thinking about living. In contrast we spend lots of our energy as grown-ups thinking about how to act—how to live in the world. We're concerned about the consequences of our actions-especially how others will evaluate our actions and what they'll think of us. We try to estimate whether honesty or dishonesty will get us what we want. Since these are hard estimations to make accurately, we sometimes remain suspended for long periods—afraid to take any action. And sometimes the action we finally take isn't very effective because it's not taken with conviction. We've already put too much effort into trying to predict or control the outcome. Or we're still ambivalent about whether or not to be honest, and this shows in our actions. In a real sense we're bounded by our shoulds and oughts, our belief systems, and our awareness of our needs in relation to others.

The energy and excitement common to every two year old is also available to every one of us at any age. In order to tap into it, we have to give up some of our adult ways of living and become more child-like (honest). This is no easy task.

I'm not suggesting that you be totally honest with everyone. That won't work for two reasons. First, you can't do it. Most of us have been dishonest for so long, it's more than second-nature. It's the only way we know how to be. We don't do it deliberately. It's just a habit. We're not even totally honest with ourselves.

Second, everyone doesn't want your total honesty. The key is to be appropriately honest in all your relationships. Don't try to tell it all and don't disclose indiscriminately. Choose what's important in each of your relationships and be completely honest about those things.

Peggy:

James wasn't the only one who hadn't been completely honest. I had completely blocked out my infatuation with Alex during the early years of our marriage. Even when James openly acknowledged all his affairs, I never mentioned my own temptation years ago. It wasn't that I deliberately withheld it. I had so completely blocked it out of my mind—it was as if it never happened. It was several days after James opened up to me before I remembered that experience and told him about it. He was absolutely astounded, having never suspected anything. And I must say I was astounded too, that I had suppressed any recollection of it at the time James told me about his experiences—as if one had nothing to do with the other. It did, in fact, give me some basis for understanding how James had rationalized some things and blocked other things he didn't want to face. I didn't want to admit I'd ever been so tempted, but I believe it was invaluable in helping me understand how it's possible to be attracted to someone else after you're married.

James:
I really felt funny when Peggy told me about her thing with Alex. It was nothing compared to all I'd done, but I still had this foolish feeling. To think I'd been so naive. I'd considered him one of my best friends. The idea of his trying to go to bed with Peggy was the furthest thing from my mind.

Peggy:
Another important change took place within the same week James told me about his affairs. He decided to stop drinking liquor. He said it was because he wanted to stay more clear-headed for discussions. I thought it was related to his decision to hold off on affairs for the time being. I thought drinking had always been a part of setting the mood for chasing women.

James:
I didn't think of my decision to quit as connected to my opening up to Peggy. I'd been thinking about the amount I was drinking for the past six months. This was stimulated by discussions with a friend and by a number of instances where participants in workshops I was running had drunk themselves out of commission. I really enjoyed the light

feeling that comes from being pleasantly intoxicated. Peggy had expressed concern several times during the past five years that I was drinking too much. Each time I quickly dismissed her remarks. I saw myself as being able to handle liquor well and I had no intention of ever letting it get out of control.

Once I started to look honestly at my drinking, several things were obvious. I was in a pattern of consuming more and more. This trend was very clear over the past seven or eight years. I never lost control or drank myself into oblivion, but I was constantly pressing the limits—at social cocktail parties and drinking with the guys at workshops. I was good at judging just how long and how much I could drink and still function the next day. But it wasn't taking me anywhere good. I decided I'd rather stop altogether than just cut back. It was probably a life-saving decision for me.

Peggy:
My mind was extremely active during this period. I tried to get control over my thoughts by writing down my feelings. Here's a sample from my journal:

My emotions constantly change. Most of the time I'm happier than I could ever imagine being. Then sometimes, without any warning, I get a feeling washing over me that this is all a dream. It seems terribly unreal I get warm behind the ears and my head feels giddy. I feel a rush of realization of all that's happened and it almost overwhelms me.

I resent the way James manipulated me all those years. He used my need for approval to keep me in line. His attitude was one that said "Don't give me any of your fears or you 'll get rejected " I've had a pit in my stomach ever since I realized the sheer magnitude of his willingness to allow me to be hurt.

I keep trying to find ways to diminish the hurt. Whenever I begin to think about James having sex with all those women I try to pretend we weren't married at the time. That way it isn't quite as painful I feel good when I stay in the present. But I have a kind of haunting feeling—a longing deep inside—that the past would go out of my mind completely. It's painful to think of the past seven years in light of the new information about his activities during that time. Everything seems somehow affected by the deception. Learning so much at once has made it seem as significant as if it had all happened at once. It alters my memory of just about everything. I wonder how he could have been involved in some particular event with me while a part of him was involved with another woman.

The result is that I keep trying to block out the past. Since I don't think I can succeed in denying the past seven years, I'm forcing myself to focus on them. I need to reconcile myself to living with all this information. And I think the best way to do it is to go along with the pain and find out how I can deal with it. I need to start trying to fit all this information into place—to understand it—not keep it buried It simply won't stay buried anyway. It would just eat me up if I tried

I'm aware of how much easier it is to "understand" all this than to accept it emotionally. I have to keep living life and dealing with other people. I find I want to avoid contact with people who knew about the affairs. There are so many reminders in so many places, I at least want to avoid being reminded by the presence of others who had first-hand knowledge.

Thank goodness none of the women were friends of ours or in our social circle. That would have been almost too much to bear. There are, nevertheless, a number of his men friends who knew it all along. To my surprise this is not the kind of thing men hide from one another. In fact, it's widely accepted It seems to be a kind of secret society whose membership is open to all males. Because of James' openness and candidness with me, I an now aware that this secret society exists. I think most women have no idea how

Facing The Truth

open men are with each other about their affairs. It's difficult to realize so many men understand, accept, and in some cases even encourage the idea of affairs.

The burning question for me in all this continues to be, "Why." What caused him to have affairs" He's tried to explain his rationale, but I just can't understand it. I keep asking, "Why Why Why" I realize it won't change anything, but I need to make sense out of all this. I just can't make the part of him I didn't know fit with the part I did know all those years.

He's explained to me about the influence of seeing other men involved in outside sex. And he's explained about the natural sex drive. But I keep looking for enough reasons to outweigh the risk of losing me and the kids. I think it boils down to the fact that he never acknowledged the risk he was taking. He just figured he "wouldn't get caught."

James:

Sometimes it irritated me that Peggy kept coming back to the same question, "Why?" I didn't appreciate that this was really a reflection of the depth of her ultimate reaction. I had been misled by her seemingly easy acceptance of the whole thing that first night I opened up to her. I kept telling her it had nothing to do with her. I did it because it was there to be done. It was fun, exciting, satisfying. From observing other men, I'd come to believe it was the natural thing to do. None of this satisfied Peggy. She would wait a few days and ask again, "Why?"

She was really saying, "What's wrong with me and our marriage?" She had bought what is still the most widely held assumption about why people have affairs. Namely, that there's a problem in the marriage. No doubt, problems in the marriage do lead some spouses to have affairs, but I think this has been overestimated as the primary cause. I started having affairs soon after I noticed a lot of other men doing it. I didn't start immediately because the idea was too foreign to me. I had to shift a few things around in my head. That didn't take long. Within a few months after I became aware of the prevalence of affairs, I was an eager participant.

Nothing had gone wrong with our marriage, and I was not trying to "get at" Peggy in any way. I was simply trying to get in on what I thought looked like a good thing. It was a good thing in part, but it was a lot more complicated than it appeared on the surface.

I've talked with enough other men to think I am not unusual on this issue. It leads me to believe that monogamy is not man's natural state. Or more directly, being married doesn't stop a man or woman from feeling attracted to a member of the opposite sex. And even having a good marriage doesn't stop some from acting on their feelings.

One of the things I came to value most about having affairs was the novelty. The excitement of making it with a new partner the first time is hard to match. I wish I knew how to reproduce that in an ongoing relationship. I know what the books say, but going to a motel or introducing some exotic twist just doesn't do the same thing for me. I'm not saying you shouldn't try new things to keep excitement in an ongoing relationship. BY all means, do it. It does help. Just don't expect miracles. In my experience, that fever pitch of tension and excitement exists only once in any relationship. It lasted longer in my first affair, but then with each succeeding one, the duration was shorter and shorter.

We all want to have new experiences in some parts of our lives. I think I became addicted to novelty in sex—the excitement of the unknown. Men who have known only one woman sexually often have difficulty understanding this. Some have said to me, "What's the point? They all have the same equipment. Once you've had one woman you've had them all." A man who makes such a statement has either had sex with only one woman, none at all, or he has an extremely low level of awareness. The gross anatomy is the same, but every person is unique, as any experienced lover will tell you.

Facing The Truth

I think this was the only area where my sex with Peggy came up short in comparison with the sex in my affairs. And it wasn't a fair comparison. Once I was past the novelty, none of the outside sex I had was better than what I had with Peggy. I'm making all these comments from the male perspective because it's the only one I know from the inside. I believe many of the same things are true for a woman looking at her sexual experience with men.

The only other reason I could come up with to the question of why was curiosity. Once I knew about it, I wanted to see what it was like firsthand. But I don't believe I could have acted on my curiosity if I hadn't seen several powerful role models doing it. That gave me permission to violate the societal shoulds and oughts I'd grown up with. I'm not trying to justify my behavior. I'm trying to understand and describe it. Had I never seen a person I liked and admired having affairs, I feel sure my experience would have been different. My curiosity was stimulated not just by looking at women in isolation, but by seeing married men involved in outside sex.

Peggy:

There were a couple of insights I'd gained that I didn't want to lose. I decided to write them down as a reminder of what was important to me in all this.

First, I want to look on my marriage and the hopes I have for it not in terms of duties, obligations, and expectations. I want to think of my relationship in terms of two people who are voluntarily committed to each other. I want our guidelines to be the ones we follow because we choose them, not because they are imposed upon us.

Second, I want to remember that our current relationship is what's important. The time we've invested in our marriage is only worth whatever satisfactions we have now. It doesn't help to spend a lot of time thinking about the past. I know "you can't go back"--and I wouldn't want to. Not that there aren't things I'd like to change. But any major changes would affect some of the good things that are also a part of the past.

I sometimes long to be able to go back and change my attitude toward myself and toward our relationship. I think I was short-sighted in putting our relationship first. I devoted all my energies to "us," thinking that would ensure James doing the same. I thought I could control his behavior by controlling my own and sacrificing myself as a person.

James:
I began to feel in our early years of marriage that Peggy's "you first" stance wasn't a good thing for either of us. I didn't have a very clear understanding of all that was involved. Mainly, I thought she was giving up too much of herself and someday she'd resent me for it. Having the kids compounded the problem as James saw it. I don't think I ever comprehended the sense of responsibility she felt for them on a continuing basis. In trying to get her to be less responsible and less self-denying, she saw me as irresponsible. The net result was she thought she had to be more responsible to make up for me. It's a pity we didn't have better skills for dealing with our differences in those days. We inadvertently pushed each other to opposite ends of the continuum. We were both the losers as a result.

On the outside Peggy has always looked like a happy, effective person. I think most of her friends and acquaintances over the years would describe her as bright, talented in many areas, and successful at most things she tried. On the inside she's been far from happy. She has been extremely critical of herself. In her own view she never quite measured up. She was never as pretty, as religious, as good a singer, daughter, wife, mother, tennis player, etc., as she "knew" she could be or ought to be. Despite her obvious successes, Peggy didn't see herself as a winner.

I think the main reason for this discrepancy had to do with the specific activities she engaged in. Throughout her life she's invested a lot of energy in what society and others have said she ought to do—not what she wanted to do. Being successful at what others say is good to do is a poor second to doing what you want. Not that she didn't get some enjoyment out of her "societal successes." She did. But her predominant feeling has been one of deprivation—giving up what she wanted in favor of what others said she ought to have.

For too long Peggy's life had been out of balance, and she'd felt powerless to take direct steps to change it. She'd been too dependent on me, and the kids had been too dependent on her because of my low availability to them. The result was, she felt smothered and trapped, unable to have enough independent control of her own time.

I think Peggy's lifestyle was typical of millions of American women who live out the roles prescribed by society. To her, being a good wife and mother too often meant submerging her wants and needs in favor of mine and the kids. She learned to do it well, but she never liked it. Sometimes her anger and resentment would build to the point that she would express it toward me, accusing me of being selfish and inconsiderate of her and others. More often, she would direct it inward and the result was depression. In the early years of our marriage I thought she was just doing what any good wife would do. I'd been conditioned to hold the same values. My own mother was a beautiful example of a woman who consistently put the family's needs in front of her own and claimed to be completely happy with her role.

Peggy:

Historically, the role of "wife and mother" has been glorified by our society, but there hasn't been real recognition and respect for the challenging job it represents. I believe homemakers are the most unappreciated of all women today because of the emphasis in our society on the ability to earn money. We have somehow confused self-worth with monetary worth. The role of the homemaker is one of the most complex, demanding jobs a person can have. A clear focus on the value of that role should inspire self-esteem in the women who handle it so capably. But society hasn't supported this view. The attitudes toward homemakers fail to acknowledge the day-to-day strength, competence, and versatility that are required to do the job well.

Many women are like me in that they never fully recognize and appreciate the extent of their capabilities. They often take for granted all the complicated tasks and responsibilities they handle routinely. While no specific credentials are required to perform the homemaker's role, the skills in management, counseling, coordinating, scheduling, planning, goal-setting, decision-making, and finance rival those skills needed to run a business organization.

For years I never appreciated my ability as demonstrated by being a full-time wife and mother. I felt somehow "less" because I was not employed outside the home. The term "just a housewife" implies some sort of apology for not being "more. " I've come to see it's not the job itself that needs to be more. It's the honest recognition of its importance that needs to be increased. Many of us knock ourselves out trying to be "perfect" to prove we are indispensable. When this superhuman effort is not fully appreciated, we are likely to be resentful. After all, "Look how hard I tried." Depression is likely to follow. I suffered from depression for years over my unsuccessful efforts to "prove myself."

I didn't like the way I compared with James in my own eyes or in the eyes of others. He always seemed more important and whatever he had to say seemed more important. I think a lot of this "importance" has been determined in our society based on income-producing activities vs. non-income-producing activities. James (and other men) can discuss issues related to work that are unquestionably accepted as important. After all, this work produces income. A homemaker who discusses issues related to her job at home may be seen as griping about unimportant things or may be turned off and not listened to because she "can't talk about anything but the house and kids." We need to recognize that other values are at least as important as earning money. If we get these values straight, then the homemaker discussing "home" issues would be recognized as just as important as the worker discussing "work" issues. But while I was a homemaker I failed to see through the bind I was in as a woman in our society.

I must admit I felt better about myself once I went back to "work" (earning money). But it wasn't completely satisfying because I often felt guilty at not being a stay-at-home mother. That's part of the double-bind for women. If we are full-time homemakers we feel defensive about being "just a housewife." If we are working mothers we feel guilty for not being a full-time housewife. During different periods of time the pressure has changed from one to the other. During the 50's most of the pressure was on the career woman to feel guilty for not being a full-time homemaker. Later this shifted so that the full-time homemaker became pressured to feel guilty for not having a career. Hopefully, we are moving toward an attitude that accepts the idea of a woman doing what is right for her at any given time in her life.

James:

From the summer of 1970 (when Peggy went back to work) through January of 1974 (when I decided to be honest with her) Peggy's self-image improved substantially. My telling her about my affairs brought a new sense of urgency to this whole process. It crystallized some things that had been forming in her thinking. She saw clearly that the subservient role she had adopted in relation to me had not worked. The same night I told her, she decided to start respecting her own needs and acting in her own behalf more often. There was a grim determination in her voice when she told me this the next morning. She looked me straight in the eye and said, "In the past I have filled the needs of others to a greater extent than I now feel willing to do. I want to figure out what I need to do for myself. I want to find how to define myself as a person and how to feel good about myself."

These were powerful insights for Peggy. I felt the most powerful of all was her new awareness that she needed to pay more attention to defining and meeting her own needs. I was also afraid of how that would eventually change our relationship. I wasn't eager for a complete overhaul since I liked most aspects of our marriage. But I felt it was a healthy decision for her and all of us connected to her.

In the years since Peggy made that decision, she has made great progress in regaining some of the autonomy she rightfully felt the need for. It hasn't been easy or smooth. She had to change some basic values that she had grown up with and acted on for eighteen years of our married life. She had built her life around a support role for me and the kids. At the very core of that approach is the belief that if you are good at sensing and meeting other people's needs, everything will be beautiful. It's a lovely ideal, but it doesn't work unless it's balanced with a healthy amount of self-assertion.

Peggy:

The strides I made in independence would not have been possible without James' support. I had a growing feeling that I wanted more out of life, but I felt guilty if I did things for myself. I was becoming much more aware of the restrictions I had unnecessarily placed on myself, but I found it hard to break out of my habit of self-denial. James' encouragement helped me feel OK about changing some of those habits.

Many of the events that contributed most to my growth were initiated by him. The most important factor was his including me in his work. He also asked me to attend the conference with him in Chicago and then suggested my going to the TA seminar alone, which I did just prior to his telling me about his affairs. This was just the beginning of his continuing support and encouragement for my becoming a more independent person.

James:
Living with Peggy during this period of her growing consciousness about her own role and the role of women in our society in general has been a challenge and a source of much learning for me. I was raised to be as chauvinistic as the next guy, so I had plenty of learning to do. We had similar reactions to our first exposure to the radical "lib" movement in the late 1960's. It was too far out and extreme for us to relate to. Neither of us was hurting enough or aware enough to appreciate the significance of the issues they were raising. And we were probably a little frightened by the man-hating stance some of the early radicals were taking. It didn't fit our fairytale of how things ought to be.

About 1970 we both started to pay attention and be more receptive to the messages of the women's movement. Peggy never went through the angry, revengeful stage some women do, but she's had a steadily growing awareness of the ways women have been disadvantaged in our society and what it means for a woman to assert her rights today. Learning with and from her brought some much needed balance into my life. I'd been lumping all women into a group, and this was causing me to miss a lot of the potential in my interactions with them. In particular, my stereotypical way of thinking about women was keeping me from knowing Peggy as deeply as I could. Prior to 1970 I hadn't even thought of her as a person I could learn from. January, 1974, was a definite milestone for both of us in this regard. My opening up to her signaled a new level of respect and equality in our relationship. At the same time she knew, once and for all, that she had to assume the primary responsibility for meeting her needs. The fairytale was over.

BEYOND AFFAIRS

Peggy:

I was only one of many women who were learning that the fairytale was over—that in fact it had never existed. It's important as women that we come to grips with the fact that ultimately each of us is responsible for ourselves. Our children grow up, our husbands die, or a divorce may leave us on our own. A look at statistics on divorce and on lifespans of men and women makes it clear most women will someday be alone. Our self-image and self-confidence will be all we have.

This self-confidence is also essential in dealing with affairs. My increased appreciation of my own worth as a person separate from my role as James' wife was an important factor in my ability to hear this kind of news. I was a much stronger person than in the early days of his affairs. It's important that this kind of disclosure be done when a woman is prepared to deal with it. If it is disclosed when there has been no suspicion or recognition of the likelihood of an affair, the shock could be overwhelming. There needs to be some evidence that she wants to know. James was right in sensing my readiness. His timing was critical to my ability to hear it.

The fact that he told me voluntarily was another important factor. But just as important was his reason for telling me. He wanted to make things better—not just "get it off his chest." The man who admits he's having an affair in order to clear his conscience or relieve his guilt may be giving his wife more than she can bear. Had I not been prepared for the facts after so many years of suspecting and had James' motives not been so positive—I feel sure my reaction would have been significantly different. I would have been angry, shocked, probably hysterical, and most certainly vindictive.

If a woman feels insecure and is shocked by the news, her pride may be so wounded that she will feel compelled to get a divorce. If she feels inadequate to make it on her own, especially with children, she may face a difficult choice. The

Facing The Truth

decisions-"to tell" or "not to tell" and "to divorce" or "not to divorce"—can only be made by the people involved.

Another major area affected by an affair is trust. Trust has been broken, and rebuilding it is a difficult task. If James had refused to answer my questions, I would have continued to wonder what he wasn't telling me. I doubt that I would have trusted anything he said again. But he worked hard at earning my trust by telling me anything I wanted to know about the past. More importantly, he vowed to be completely honest with me from that point on. His words might not have been enough, but he backed them up with action.

A couple of weeks after he told me about his affairs, he acknowledged that the only unfinished business he had was to let Terry know he was "out of circulation. " It was February of 1974 and he hadn't seen her since the preceding September, but as far as she knew he would be seeing her again sometime. In order to be completely straight about all this, he needed to let her know. I know it must have been a difficult call to make, but it meant a great deal to me that he did it. He explained everything to her. She wasn't surprised. She had suspected I knew back in Rochester.

It was clear that by calling Terry, James was calling a halt to his past involvements. But I didn't know what was going to happen in the future because he still said he wanted both of us to be open to having affairs. I didn't want to have affairs, and I hoped he would change his mind. In the meantime, I felt somewhat in limbo. We'd been working on plans to build our first house and expected to begin construction in just three months. I wasn't at all sure we would be able to resolve this difference on having affairs, and I thought we should delay building. But James was insistent—he said he wasn't going to rush me or force me, and he was sure we could work it out.

We continued with our house plans. But I was not as confident as James that we could settle our differences about having an "open marriage."

8

Open Marriage?

James:
I thought the sexually open marriage was the coming thing and I wanted to be in the forefront. I was constantly looking for evidence to support this point of view. Sexual freedom—that's the thing. I wanted it without even knowing what it meant. I believe lots of folks want it, but I doubt if anyone has it. We've all been victimized by hundreds of cultural do's and don'ts about sexual behavior very early in life—before we were able to evaluate for ourselves how much sense they made.

Many of these early learnings stick with us for life. Others are modified by the addition of new information from friends and our own personal experience. Puberty brings an explosion of sexual feelings and a new need to know—what it's about and what to do with it. For many of us, it's a frustrating time. Nature has given us the capacity, but society tells us to wait. "Wait until you're married or finished with your education, preferably both." Society never stops telling us how it ought to be. The problem is, many of the external messages are conflicting with each other and with our own desires and impulses. It's no wonder more of us are sexually frustrated than satisfied.

My early learning was clear. Marriage is forever and there's no provision for outside relationships. My experience was different. Sex with others is fun, exciting, and satisfying. What I wanted was to find an authority figure Peggy and I both respected who would revoke my early rules and proclaim some new ones. Many people thought Nena and George O'Neill were doing just that in their best-selling book, Open Marriage. They were suggesting an alternative to the traditional, closed marriage most of us have, but their "open marriage" did not necessarily include outside sex. They were careful to say a couple that had developed an open marriage based on honesty and equality ought to be able to include outside sex without the usual feelings of jealousy and envy, but they were not specifically recommending it. It was simply an option. I searched high and low, but I never found an "authority" who clearly recommended it.

Peggy:
I desperately wanted the reassurance that we would not include outside relationships. I didn't have any regrets about having been monogamous. Our sex life was so good that I couldn't see how it made sense to have affairs. In fact, I could never have imagined what a difference our new openness would make in the way we related to each other sexually. I can't explain just why this happened. I do know it had something to do with the closeness created by our commitment to honesty.

The togetherness I felt was more like "oneness" when we lay in each other's arms following sex. I often felt lifted up and floated around in space. The invisible barrier created

Open Marriage?

by the secrecy and deception of the past was no longer between us. We were more vulnerable to each other and more caring and considerate. Feelings of love flowed stronger than ever before. We developed a new openness to showing our desires and pleasures.

We didn't focus on any new sex techniques or other sexual efforts. But our openness with each other led to a tremendous increase in both the quantity and quality of our sex. I began having more orgasms, and they were significantly different from the past. I'd read a lot about "bigger and better orgasms" and "vaginal vs. clitoral orgasms," but had never had much confidence in what I read. When I began having orgasms that involved my whole body—not just my genitals—I was amazed.

In the past I had felt throbbing contractions in my genitals and more excited breathing patterns at the time of orgasm. Now I was having other reactions as well. For example, my nipples would get hard and erect and I would bead with perspiration on my back and neck. These reactions were obvious. I couldn't possibly have faked them in the way I faked orgasms years ago. Thank god I no longer felt like I had to pretend.

I still didn't always have an orgasm; but when I didn't, I was honest about it. I learned I could have one anytime I let myself pursue whatever felt most exciting to me. That meant taking charge of the lovemaking more often. I found I was much more in control when I was on top during intercourse, and with that control I could get whatever pleasure I wanted. James got more pleasure too because of my added enjoyment. It took the pressure off him to "do it for me."

There are too many myths and bad jokes about women's sexuality that have affected us in a negative way. The old "not tonight, I have a headache" line is one of the more ridiculous of these. The truth is that nothing is better for relieving a headache than good sex. Most headaches are tension-related. The release of tension through sex is an effective cure for a headache. And it sure beats "taking two aspirin."

    I labored under many of the same illusions about female sexuality that other women held before we began sharing the truth with each other. (The Hite Report clarified a lot of this and allowed us to acknowledge what we've known in our hearts all along about our sexuality. It helped us break through the unrealistic patterns of lovemaking we had accepted.) All those years of lying on my back in the "dead bug" position, expecting to be satisfied, were behind me. I felt more confidence in myself and more willingness to assert myself and show my needs and preferences. I think I was strongly affected by being treated like an equal for the first time in my life. I no longer intended to be passive in my sex life or in other areas.

    I especially had no intention of subjecting myself to living in a double standard again. If James continued to have affairs, I felt I would have to come to terms with some way to have them myself—or I'd have to get out of the relationship. James wanted me to have an affair in order to see that I could do it without affecting my love or commitment to him. I had never been able to understand how his affairs had not affected his love for me. But I couldn't see having one myself just to understand it. I was in a terrible dilemma. I was trying to keep an open mind. I was willing to consider he might be right—but I couldn't imagine who I could have an affair with. I felt there were so many restrictions. I would want it to be someone I really cared for as a person and someone I was attracted to. I wouldn't want it to be one of James' personal friends or professional colleagues. And I wouldn't want to get involved with a man who was married. It seemed highly unlikely I'd find someone who overcame all these restrictions.

    I was pushing myself to think through all this and make a decision. I felt a great need to get things settled—one way or the other. I knew we might not be able to work this out and I might be on my own. I thought if that were to happen,

Open Marriage?

I'd want it to be sooner rather than later. I didn't want to stay in this limbo situation. I couldn't see going along this way for maybe five or ten years before making a decision either to get a divorce or have a sexually open marriage. I was already thirty-eight years old. I realized as a female in our society age would be a decided factor in making it on my own, either professionally or sexually. I hoped we could decide on monogamy, but if we couldn't, then I'd rather acknowledge it before I got any older.

My increased awareness of "women's issues" as they related to me led me to be somewhat self-contained and not completely vulnerable to James. I felt a need to hold back a little to protect myself in the event we didn't make it. I knew I'd need all the strength and independence I could muster. I was determined to be treated fairly and to protect myself from being hurt again in the way I was hurt in the past—and the way I was still hurting from the past.

James:

There were times when I thought we wouldn't make it. We'd seem to be making progress, and then Peggy would get in touch with some memories that depressed her and put us right back to ground zero. It was frustrating for both of us. She wanted to let go of the past and move on as much as I did, but we couldn't seem to get beyond these nagging questions.

I would go over and over the way I had gradually come to accept that having affairs was the thing to do from observing my peers and role models. I would describe as best I could the intricate rationalization process that allowed me to carry on the deceit without feeling guilty. But it was never enough. It always had a hollow, intellectual ring to it. We spent many an hour working on this with roughly the same outcome-Peggy feeling something was missing and me feeling frustrated that she couldn't understand or accept my explanation.

BEYOND AFFAIRS

I think she knew intuitively what the problem was, but she was unable to get it through to me. An important part of maintaining my image of myself as an OK person entailed not looking at the world from Peggy's point of view. That would have been too painful. My avoidance of that perspective for seven years was so complete that I was really convinced my actions had not been that hurtful to her. When she told me how much anxiety and pain she had experienced, I said I was sorry, but I wasn't really aware of the depth of her feelings. I had been avoiding facing them for too long to really see them.

The old "what she doesn't know can't hurt her" philosophy was the cornerstone of my belief system. While I was having affairs, I was convinced it was true. I am amazed at my ability to rationalize my actions and compartmentalize my values so I didn't have any internal conflict with what I was doing.

I had colluded with other men on a continuing basis to maintain the charade. We enjoyed recounting our affairs to each other—especially the ones where there was some element of risk. Almost being discovered was sure to etch an affair in memory forever. The real key was to be able to end the story in the right way—having engaged in the affair without getting caught. This was the way men of the world did it. And any man who couldn't handle an affair with an appropriate display of "cool" was suspect—not yet developed and mature.

The more I talked about affairs with Peggy, the more convinced I became that I wanted to continue having them and that I could cope with her having them too. I consistently told her in a low-key way that I was open to that. I thought it might help her understand some of the positive things I had experienced. I also believed that was the only way I could be free to have affairs again. With this in mind, I encouraged Peggy to attend a conference on sexuality in August, 1974, in New York state. I was running a workshop in Pittsburgh the same week, so we drove up

Open Marriage?

together. She dropped me off on Sunday and drove on to the conference. Before we parted, I told her again it would be all right with me if she had a sexual relationship with another man whenever she chose.

Peggy:

The sexuality conference was geared toward helping counselors, therapists, and clergymen deal with various sexual issues encountered in their professional roles. One of the subjects to be covered at the conference was "open marriage." This was the main reason I was going. I was trying to understand how this was possible and how James could be in favor of it.

I had put an enormous amount of effort into the process of considering an affair. I would think about it and try to visualize it. It made me nervous, but the more I thought about it the more possible it seemed. I think this is typical of the way people change their values and their actions. You start by thinking about something until you can finally see yourself doing it. I couldn't quite see myself doing it yet, but I was certainly putting a lot of time and effort into thinking about it.

On the first evening at the conference I checked the meeting schedule specifically to see when the session on open marriage would be held and who would be leading it. I felt a need to check out the leader to see if he looked weird in any way. I had terrible misgivings about the whole thing. I saw his name listed on the schedule and kept a close watch on name tags all evening to see if I could spot him.

The evening began with dinner. A dance was scheduled afterward. This was therapeutic for me, considering the way I enjoy dancing. I relaxed somewhat from the pressure I'd been feeling about my "mission" to learn about open marriage. Just when I'd finally given up looking for the workshop leader, someone came and spoke to the guy I was dancing with—and it was the man I'd been looking for all night. I was excited at finally finding him and quickly asked if we could talk. He was surprised by the intensity of my greeting, but was quite willing to talk with me.

We left the dance and walked around the campus where the conference was being held. I described my situation with James and my concerns about the open sexual relationship he was proposing. Max told me about his relationship with his wife and how their sexually open marriage worked. We talked for three or four hours, and I poured out all my feelings. I was talking to him like I'd never talked to anyone about this. We were walking as we talked, occasionally stopping to rest. Once when we stopped, he kissed me. I was both surprised and pleased. I had been so caught up in the discussion that my feelings had sneaked up on me. I realized I was attracted to him. He was several years younger than me and one of the best looking men I had ever seen. I was flattered that he was also attracted to me.

This drastically changed things. The subject we had been discussing became a real-life situation. I could feel myself moving toward the idea of having sex with him. But I wasn't ready to move quite that fast. I still felt too uneasy and uncertain. I left him and went to bed, but I didn't sleep. I lay awake all night questioning myself, "Do you really want to do this?" "Does James really want you to?" I was scared but excited at the same time. I decided the only thing to do was call James the next morning, tell him about the situation, and ask how he felt.

James:
Peggy called Tuesday morning to say she had met someone she was interested in and to check one last time about my willingness for her to have an affair. I should have paid attention to my heart, which immediately started to beat about three times its normal rate. But I paid attention to my head instead and said, "Sure, go ahead. I've been saying it's OK and I want you to experience that for yourself."

As soon as we finished our conversation and I hung up the phone, my stomach immediately turned into a knot. I

Open Marriage?

was not at all prepared for the emotional reaction I was to have for the next two and a half days. I had thought about her being with another man in an abstract sort of way, but I had not visualized it and "felt" it. I guess part of me thought it was such a remote possibility that it probably wouldn't happen. I think I was also just plain naive. I had looked at affairs from such a one-sided point of view, I couldn't see the other side.

Peggy:
James reassured me he wanted me to feel free to decide for myself. He thought my having this experience might help me understand his attitude toward affairs. I couldn't understand how he could be so rational and unemotional about the possibility of my having sex with another man. Knowing the pain his affairs had caused me, it just didn't make sense. I knew he wanted to resume having affairs himself and wanted me to do it for that reason. But I didn't feel he was pushing me—just leaving it up to me to decide.

I was still trying to be rational about all this. So I made a "decision" to go ahead. I told Max at breakfast I had decided we could be together. He surprised me by suggesting I not make a calculated decision. He said I should just go with my feelings. That stopped me cold. I didn't know what I felt—except confused.

I participated in the conference that morning, but my mind wasn't on the sessions. Max and I were in the same body movement group, and that just heightened the awareness I had of him and of my dilemma. I had an unreal feeling. Here I was with my husband's permission and an attractive, available guy. I felt like somebody standing at the edge of the high diving board trying to decide whether to dive off or walk back down.

At noon I couldn't eat. I sat with Max and tried to be light and pleasant. But I felt like someone on a serious mission. The session on open marriage was scheduled for the afternoon. I walked in ready to discuss my dilemma fully with the other participants. I did not, however, identify Max as my potential partner. After all, he was leading the session, and I didn't want to make it more difficult for him.

    I took my turn at telling my story and listened carefully to everything the others had to say. I was looking for something I could hold onto to "make my decision for me." And it happened. (I think we commonly do that—look for somebody or something to make it OK for us to decide whatever it is we want to do.) By now I really wanted to have an affair with Max, but I was afraid I'd regret it and needed some reassurance I wouldn't. Sure enough, one of the people in the group said, "Your reaction to it is completely within your power. You don't have to wait to see whether or not you'll regret it. If you decide it'll be OK, it will be OK." Then and there I decided to do it.

    It seemed to be the natural, even appropriate, thing to do under the total circumstances. I doubt I could have reached this conclusion in a different setting, but the minute the session ended I was clear about going ahead. I was so nervous, I was actually shaking.

    I went up to Max and said, "Take me somewhere and hold me before I fall apart." He had been right about advising me to get in touch with my feelings instead of trying to make a cold decision. But neither of us was prepared for the intensity of the feelings I would have. I think it must have been contagious, because by the time we had walked to his room, he had started shaking too. Then I didn't feel so strange. (I discovered he had been with only a couple of other women, even though he had a sexually open marriage.) He stopped to ask if I were protected from pregnancy before we began to make love. I had an IUD, but I was touched by his thoughtfulness at a time when I was unable to think at all.

    The sex was so good and the feelings so positive, I could hardly believe it. I felt like a child again—free and happy. It seemed unreal and at the same time very natural. After all, I had my husband's blessings and felt I was doing something good, both for me and for our marriage. I gave myself over fully to the situation. Time seemed to stand still. It was late afternoon and the sun was streaming in the windows as we lay there and talked for hours. We also laughed a lot. I was really pleased with myself. I started singing, "If My Friends Could See Me Now." I felt like shouting to the world about the "new me." It was like discovering another person who had been locked inside until now.

Finally, time imposed other demands. Max and I each had separate meetings to attend that night. But we began to make love again before we had to go. Then, of all things, there was a knock on the door and a key started to turn in the lock. He had been assigned a roommate who had arrived a day late. We jumped apart with a flurry as he yelled for the guy to wait a minute. Then he went to the door and asked him to please come back in a few minutes. I was standing behind the door, about to burst in giggles. Normally, I would have been mortified by such a situation and would have felt terribly guilty and embarrassed. I don't know how to convey just how amazing this kind of behavior was for me. But it was contradictory to any reaction I'd ever had to a situation that could potentially be embarrassing. Somehow everything just seemed so right that nothing seemed to make any difference. The guy left and we resumed our lovemaking—then laughingly got dressed and parted to go to our meetings.

As I sat in my meeting a little while later, I heard whistling coming from the hall. Then I recognized it was Max whistling "If My Friends Could See Me Now." He walked back and forth several times, while I tried to keep a straight face.

We hadn't intended to get together again after the meeting. Since I'd had no sleep the night before, I planned to go to bed early. But one look at him and I knew sleep would have to wait. Since he had a roommate now, and so did I, there seemed to be nowhere to go to be alone. Finally, we got in my car and decided to drive around to see if we could find a place to park. That resulted in some of the funniest scenes I've been part of in years. Here we were looking for a place to park, just like teenagers. We drove a few miles into the country, but still couldn't find a place that seemed reasonable. Through all this driving and looking, we were getting more and more impatient. It was hard to drive under those conditions. We finally gave up and went back to the conference site and made love in the car—right there in the parking lot. The nervousness of being detected just added to the excitement. It really was reminiscent of high school days. It seemed impossible to be recapturing such a feeling of youth after feeling grown-up and responsible for so many years.

I was getting an understanding of one reason James had valued his affairs so much. I could now see firsthand some of the benefits he had gained from them. Affairs represent newness and variety. They stand for youth and excitement and freedom and fun.

James had been impressed with the "playfulness" of some of the women he had affairs with, and I'd felt serious by comparison. I now realized the person involved in an affair—man or woman—presents a side of themselves that is not fully representative of the whole person. It's a special version of their freshest and best aspects. I believe it's not the specific person who is either serious or playful, but which role you happen to be in at the time. When I'm in the "wife" role, I have a lot of responsibilities and distractions connected with that role. When I'm in the "lover" role, I have no responsibilities or distractions from being fun-loving and playful. The same is likely to be true of any other person.

I saw another potential benefit of affairs. Much of the attraction that exists is the reflection of yourself you get through the other person's eyes. Through them you are able to see yourself as more youthful, sexual, interesting, and desirable. It's easy to see what a boon it can be to your confidence and self-esteem. I now understood why James

Open Marriage?

always had such a good self-image. It was getting fed regularly by this view of himself through the eyes of other women. My self-esteem had been dependent on the reflection I got through his eyes—without this additional boost from other men.

I realized these were some of the things James wanted me to understand and part of the reason he wanted me to have this experience. It did give me a basis for understanding how his affairs had been valuable for him as a person without interfering with his feelings for me. But it still amazed me that he didn't mind my being with someone else. I didn't see how anyone could handle their partner having an affair without feeling some pain.

Max had tried to describe to me the way he and his wife dealt with this. He said he had a deep commitment to her and it hurt him terribly when she was with someone else (as it hurt her when he was), but they were not willing to deny each other the pleasure to be found in their outside affairs. In talking about their relationship, I got a clear understanding of how much pain was involved along with the freedom. I asked him if his freedom was really worth the pain. He said it wasn't just his freedom he valued. He wanted his wife to be free and happy and would do whatever necessary to allow her that freedom. It sounded great in theory, but I couldn't imagine actually choosing to undergo the pain of knowing your spouse was with someone else. James seemed to be willing to accept the pain...or not to feel it. I knew I'd still have a lot of work to do before I could accept it.

I put these thoughts aside for the time being and just enjoyed my new freedom. I slept like a log that night and felt great the next morning. I literally floated through the day, attending sessions and meeting people. I felt so good about everything and everybody. And most of all, I felt good about myself.

BEYOND AFFAIRS

Max and I met during the day between sessions and planned to get together at the end of the day. It was August and very hot. So we decided to take a walk to a nearby lake. We stopped and talked to some children on the way. One little boy looked a lot like his son. We showed each other pictures of our families and talked about them. Vicki and Andy were at camp for two weeks. Max's children, who were younger, were at home with his wife.

He said his wife fully expected he would be involved with someone at the conference. We talked for hours about the pleasures and pain of a sexually open marriage. It seemed amazing to me, but I was beginning to believe it must be possible. It was beautiful by the lake and we didn't want to leave, but it was about to get dark. As we walked back to the conference, we started thinking about what we might do that night. I remembered we weren't far from Rochester, where we had once lived. I knew of a nice hotel built on a nearby lake. We decided to dress and go there for dinner—not planning anything definite beyond that. I usually liked to have things more controlled and planned, but Max was clear about our just doing whatever seemed right at the moment. It felt exciting to be on an adventure—not knowing just where it would lead.

Dinner was beautiful, but I didn't eat much. I was too caught up in the whole experience to pay much attention to the food. We had a lovely view of the lake from the dining room. The whole setting felt like something out of a fairytale.

By the time we finished dinner we knew we wanted to check into the hotel. I can't imagine where I got the nerve, but I went up to the desk and registered for us. I signed in as Max and Peggy Vaughan—as if Max had my last name. I used my credit card, and it was very simple. (It felt great to be doing this on my own. Whenever I was with James, he always handled such things.) Max went to the car to get a hanging bag I had in the trunk—so we would look respectable checking in. The bag didn't have any of my

Open Marriage?

things in it. It was filled with my kids' clothes. But it made me feel better...and I thought it was terribly funny.

We had not decided whether we would stay all night. Again, we were going to wait to see how we felt—not try to decide ahead of time. Once in the room, we made love and talked for hours. He was an excellent lover—not surprising since he had been conducting workshops on sexuality for the past couple of years. But it wasn't his expertise that mattered; it was his caring and sensitivity.

He allowed himself to be vulnerable to me by telling me his concerns about his image, his relationships, and other aspects of his life. Since I was so vulnerable to him, it felt good to have a two-way sharing.

The hours passed quickly. We had no desire to part, so we settled in to spend the night. When I started to go to sleep I moved over to my side of the bed, but he wanted me to sleep right next to him all night. Spending the night with another woman was a new experience for him, and he felt it was very special. That made me feel terrific. I could see why he didn't want to decide these things ahead of time.

The next morning we took a shower together and made love one last time—there in the shower. We took more time than we had planned, and it became obvious we wouldn't get back to the conference in time to change clothes before attending the final total-group meeting. I had on a long dress from the night before and felt uncomfortable about going to the session in it. It was an Indian design, not a formal kind of long dress, but I felt I'd be wearing a neon sign saying I hadn't been home all night. Max encouraged me to be myself and feel natural. He assured me people would love me wearing the dress. J thought about it and was able to completely change my attitude. I remembered the words to a song..."I feel like a natural woman." I began to feel that way—natural and right. It seemed to allow me to be freer and to relate to people in a special way. Others responded to me differently too. I felt a kind of magic as I moved through the crowd at the end of the conference. I can best explain this feeling by sharing an incident. An older woman came up to me as I smiled and spoke to people. She stood in front of me, watching for awhile, then said, "Can I touch you?"

But the magic was soon to end. I got a call from James that morning as the conference closed. He had been trying to reach me all night. When the full force of what he had done in approving this affair hit him, he found it unbearable. He had not anticipated or imagined the degree of anxiety he experienced as the idea soaked in on him that I was actually with another man. When he got me on the phone, his first question was, "Are you all right?"...followed by, "Are we all right?" To both questions I gave a resounding, "Yes!"

James:
For two and a half days I had been numbed with fears of all sorts. Maybe Peggy would connect with an uncaring "bastard" and he would leave her feeling used. Maybe he would be crazy and hurt her physically. Maybe she would fall in love with him and want to leave me. I don't know which was worse—my fear of her being hurt or my fear that she would have such a good experience that it would in some way diminish what we had. I don't recall ever spending a comparable period in such misery. Fear was my constant companion. And to think I hadn't anticipated any problem at all.

Two days after I gave Peggy my OK for her involvement, I wrote the following note in my journal.

August 15, 1974
My rational mind says maybe we can cope with outside relationships.
My body has left me. I haven't tasted any of the food I put in my mouth since Tuesday. Perspective-Not knowing feels worse than anything.
I'm assuming that what I've been feeling is similar to what you have felt for the past seven years.

Open Marriage?

I now have a different sense of grief remorse—regret for what I did With my eyes open and my thinking slowed down, I trust you and trust that things will work out all right, but with my eyes closed, my fears take over and I fantasize the worst.

This has been the longest two days of my life.

Peggy:

It was Thursday noon. I had arrived at the conference Monday night. In less than three days my life had been changed—at least temporarily. I'd had a fantastic experience and was practically floating on air. James' call was a shock I hadn't anticipated. When Z finished talking, I told Max about it and said I really didn't know what to expect now. There was never any specific plan to see Max again. We lived in different parts of the country and had never talked beyond the present. But he did want me to let him know how things worked out between James and me after this surprising turn of events.

I said goodbye to Max and turned my attention to getting ready to see James. The original plan had been for me to drive to Toronto that afternoon. James would be finishing his workshop in Pittsburgh the next day and would fly to Toronto to meet me. We planned to attend a workshop there beginning the following night. But all that was changed. On the phone James said, "Come to me." He wanted me to drive straight to Pittsburgh that afternoon.

For the first time, the whole situation hit me. I felt pulled apart. I felt so good myself, but so bad to hear James' pain and fear. I also began feeling self-conscious about having had sex with another man—now that I was headed to see James. The very idea of sex with two men in the same day almost blew my mind. I symbolically made a separation between the two by doing a thorough cleansing of myself. It wasn't that I felt "dirty." I just needed some sense of separation between one man and the other. I bathed, washed my hair, shaved my legs, and douched. (I realized later that I "accidentally" left all my toilet articles in the bathroom after using them—further demonstrating the extent of my need to keep my two experiences separate.)

My mind raced even more than the car motor on the trip to Pittsburgh. I couldn't sort things out. James' reaction was such a shock. I didn't know what to expect when I got there. The closer I got, the more nervous I became. It was 9:00 p.m. by the time I finally made it. James was waiting for me.

James:
Talking to Peggy on the phone Thursday morning reduced my anxiety a little. She assured me she was fine. I still needed to see her in the flesh. Time seemed to drag as I finished the afternoon session of the workshop and waited for her to drive over from New York. When she finally got there, I felt tremendous relief. We had a good, long cry in each other's arms. There were tears of joy and tears of sadness and grief. I had never felt or acted that vulnerable with Peggy before.

This was a significant emotional event for both of us. It tore us loose from our moorings. The world as we had known it no longer existed and we had to sort things out and create a new world. It allowed both of us to see some things from the other's perspective which we hadn't been able to see before. I had not been able to see the pain Peggy had suffered in "knowing," but not knowing. Now I had a firsthand basis for understanding and we could talk about it on the same wave length. Likewise, the mystery of how I could feel so positive about affairs and still be committed to Peggy was exploded. She had a grand time with Max, but still felt totally committed to me. If anything, the affair increased her commitment. I'm not sure we could ever have broken through our beliefs and preconceived notions without this experience. Mark Twain put it this way: "A fellow who takes a bull by the tail once gets as much as sixty or seventy times the information as one who doesn't."

Open Marriage?

Peggy:
 Seeing James' pain led me to feel very protective of him. I was moved by his tenderness and caring as he carefully looked over my body to "make sure I was all right." His vulnerability sparked so much warmth and love that I wanted to comfort him and hold him close forever. I started acting on that impulse—and continued it for the entire week we were in Toronto.

James:
 It was fortunate we had planned to attend an eight-day TORI community. The essence of the TORI experience is that you join a community of people where everyone has agreed to open themselves to new levels of Trust, Openness, Realization, and interdependence—and each person is to take responsibility for meeting their own needs. It was an ideal setting for us at that time. We were both emotionally drained, but we had some fresh ways to look at our relationship and a new sense of how important it was to both of us. We were looking at the world with soft eyes. We didn't feel the need to evaluate and understand things in the way we normally do. The love we felt for each other was so powerful it was affecting the way we reacted to our total environment.

We gave ourselves permission to care for each other during the TORI experience in a way we had never done before. We had some intense, joyful, and playful sex, but I think more important were the many hours we spent softly touching, caressing, and just being with each other. We felt like gluttons...but we did it anyway.

I don't think we could have done the same thing in our back-home environment. At home two things continuously inhibit our expressions of caring for each other. The first is our pattern of working. We are both workaholics and have a pervasive feeling we ought to be doing something productive every day. So long as we have access to our typewriters, books, etc., the "need" to work seems to consistently overpower our need to care for each other. The second thing at home is our sense of responsibility in caring for the kids. There are constant timing problems as there are in any family, and we haven't dealt with them very creatively. By timing problems I am referring to the instances when we have the impulse to make love, but it's not convenient because of some activity we're engaged in with one or both kids. Their very presence in the house is to some degree an inhibition, since one of our priorities is to be available to them when they're around.

I'm not saying this is the way it has to be with either of the above issues. In fact, it's not always a problem. There are times when we are able to suspend our workaholic tendencies long enough to nourish ourselves, and there are times when we lock the bedroom door and meet our sexual needs with the kids in the house. I am saying that overall we haven't achieved a balance in our lives among these three needs—working, caring for the kids, and caring for ourselves. And I'm afraid the above order has been their actual priority, even though our intent is to value the kids and ourselves above our work.

Being physically removed from home and work enabled us to focus on each other in a different way. Another supporting factor was the climate in the TORI community. There was genuine acceptance of us and our behavior. It wasn't total. On the whole, however, the vibrations from the community were supportive. Some people simply observed and accepted us. Others took initiative in finding out what was going on with us and accepted us on that basis. All in all, it was one of the finest experiences we ever shared.

Peggy:

We developed a new closeness, a new commitment, and a new level of caring as we talked about what happened to us the week before. We touched and talked and loved and cared for each other on a constant basis. We were together—physically and emotionally—in a new way. There were no

Open Marriage?

roles, no masks, no expectations—just freedom to be together and enjoy each other.

We had never been in an environment like this one and we had never had the kind of experience personally we had just had. The combination opened us up to a lot of possibilities we would never have considered at a different time and place.

For example, there were community bathrooms (which you could avoid if you felt uncomfortable). We were practically stuck together like glue that week, so we decided to stick together in the bathroom too. Two specific incidents stand out in relation to that situation. First, the weekend community included a large number of people and was held away from our dormitory site. Therefore, we did not have access to our room...and our bed. At one point we got very anxious to have sex and couldn't think of any "private" place other than a large bathroom down the hall that wasn't being used. We found a small table to move into one of the stalls for extra comfort. We were in full swing with our sex when we heard some one enter the bathroom and go into the stall next to ours. We stayed very still and practically held our breath while they used the john and left the bathroom. We don't believe they ever knew we were there. We laughed like crazy at the idea of getting a view from the ceiling of the action in those two stalls.

James:

A more surprising incident happened later that week when the only participants were those professionals considering using TORI in their work. This part of the session was held in our dormitory building. One night when we went to the community bathroom for a shower we got into a conversation with another couple that lasted two hours. We were all in the nude. We were conscious of our nudity, but not self-conscious about

There was nothing sexual going on. We were just four people talking intently about something that interested us. I do think the nudity had an effect on the quality of our conversation. We were in essence saying, here I am—no poses or masks or facades. The nudity seemed to support a high level of candor. It was as if there were no place to hide anything; or perhaps it was a feeling that once we had allowed others to see us in that way, there wasn't any need to be other than honest in our conversation.

Peggy:
Toward the end of our time at TORI we had developed a close circle of friends, including the couple we had talked with in the bathroom. Another person in our circle was a woman who was working through a very difficult time in her marriage. Her husband was rejecting her...and she was very insecure and alone. She cried a lot as she confided her fears to us.

One night after we left her to go to bed, I continued to think about her. I felt sorry that she was alone, while we were so warm and secure. I surprised myself by thinking I would be willing to have her come lie with us to comfort her. I felt no jealousy at the idea. I even thought James would benefit by comforting someone else—since I had been comforting him all week. I asked him what he thought about it, and he said no. He cared for her as I did, but was afraid to get involved—even though it wouldn't necessarily have been sexual. I was somewhat relieved. But I wanted good things for him and for everyone else, and I felt strong enough to allow him or others whatever they wanted or needed. I was confident I could handle almost anything and that James and I would be able to work out a plan for our future together.

James:
At the end of the TORI community, we drove from Toronto to North Carolina to pick up the kids at summer camp. Even though we had to drive hard because of the tight time schedule it was still a very enjoyable trip. Being

together had a new quality for us. It didn't matter whether we were driving or lying on the beach. There was a new spark—a new interest. At one point we got so turned on sexually, we decided we didn't want to wait until night. We happened to be near Pittsburgh, so I turned off the turnpike at an exit I was familiar with and quickly found a secluded place to park. We made it in the car for the first time since our high school days. It was delightful.

It was also another chance for me to get some perspective on what Peggy had been coping with as she struggled to let go of the past. As we were screwing in the front seat, I found myself thinking that two weeks earlier she had been doing precisely the same thing with Max. Simply being in the car would trigger that memory many times. It was a weird feeling.

Peggy:
Back in our regular environment the everyday pressures and responsibilities closed in fast. I found that major changes in attitudes or feelings don't happen all at once. They develop slowly after the first steps in a new direction. This was a critical time of talking and thinking, and I felt a good bit of stress. We were questioning ourselves on where we wanted to go with our lives. Specifically, we needed to get clear on where we stood on having affairs. We kept going over and over the same points...not getting anywhere. Finally, we put our thoughts and feelings down on paper so we could analyze what all the churning emotions meant for us and our life together.

We acknowledged we had to set aside whatever others might decide was best for them—and just look at ourselves. It boiled down to two primary considerations. On the one hand, affairs were positive and enjoyable for whichever of us was involved and didn't interfere with our love and commitment to each other. On the other hand, it caused a great deal of pain for the one who was left out...and it took an enormous amount of time and effort to deal with it.

BEYOND AFFAIRS

The question came down to a matter of balance between these two factors. Does the pleasure outweigh the pain? The answer for both of us was clearly, "No." It might have been different if we hadn't been getting so much nourishment out of our relationship. Honesty had brought some new dimensions to our marriage. We felt more deeply connected than ever before. Our trust was strong and still growing. And our sex was exciting again. All these things reduced our interest in outside affairs and caused us to be reluctant to disturb what we had going. It was really a pretty simple decision once we stopped looking outside ourselves for the answer.

We felt relieved to have it settled. We'd both had a sense of urgency that was getting in our way. We'd been trying to find the ultimate answer. Once we gave up the notion that there was one, we felt comfortable with our decision and the knowledge that it was truly ours. We didn't make any vows to remain monogamous forever. We agreed it was the right choice for us at that time and acknowledged that at some other time in our lives we might decide differently. Another couple in the same circumstances might have reached a different conclusion, and theirs might have worked just as well for them.

This was clearly a milestone for us. We were now ready to get on with our lives.

9
Please Trust Me

Peggy:
The days of suffering in silence and the double standard were gone. There were still some unknowns, but they were exciting instead of anxiety-provoking. I felt good about the prospects for the future—not just in my relationship with James, but also in my work. I'd been reading and studying almost constantly during the past four years. Now it looked like it was going to begin paying off.

A few months after James opened up to me, I attended several training sessions with him. When an opportunity came for him to do some workshops for women in business, I was included as a co-trainer. For the next couple of years I was constantly receiving training myself or conducting workshops. It was a professional crash course that I absolutely loved. I had a natural ability to work with groups, and I soon became quite comfortable in functioning as a group leader. My work was not exclusively with women, but that was a large part of it.

My increasing appreciation of my own abilities carried over into my work with women. I felt all of us had sold ourselves (and each other) short. I overcame my old posture of competitiveness and began supporting them in their efforts to be successful. This new attitude came at a time when I might just as easily have developed a hatred for women—due to James' affairs. Many women become angry and bitter toward women in general, especially toward the ones involved in the affairs. That's an understandable reaction. It's easy to blame the "other woman"...as if it's all her fault. But she's only one part of the total picture.

An important factor is the opportunity that exists for affairs, especially in work or travel-related situations. Another is the support and encouragement among men in general. Any man or woman in the right place at the right time is susceptible to affairs. This was the case with James' first affair and continued to be true with later ones. I saw this for myself when I was tempted to become involved with Alex years ago. I can understand how women were attracted to James. He's always turned me on. If he were married to someone else and I were exposed to him through work or travel, I would probably still be attracted to him. I can't possibly know what I would or wouldn't do—despite my best intentions.

These understandings helped me overcome the natural tendency to think James or the other women were terrible for "doing this to me." I came to realize that we all played our part in perpetuating the situation. No man could keep his affairs from being exposed if it weren't for the cooperation he gets from both his lovers and his wife. As the wife, I never confronted James the way I could have. And the women he was with never demanded more than he was willing to give. They played according to his rules. They never exposed him in any way. They didn't confront him—or me. He was in control. "Don't call me, I'll call you" was his guideline. Even when they broke up, no woman ever called me or even threatened to. We all cooperated to protect him in his pursuit of affairs.

I feel a kind of bond with the "other woman" who is suffering in her own way with a situation over which she has little control. The wife's position in this "protective" conspiracy is somewhat understandable. But many women involved in affairs show an amazing dedication to being protective of their lovers. I know of one instance where a woman who was having an affair with a married man got pregnant by him and had an abortion without ever telling him about it.

Thank goodness, that wasn't James—but it could have been. He wasn't careful to see that the other women were protected against pregnancy. He had one experience with a one-night affair when the woman began crying after intercourse, saying she didn't have any protection. He rushed out to a drug store at midnight and bought her a douche bag. It gives me chills to think of the possibility of his getting another woman pregnant. I think that's more than I could have coped with.

I should know better than to say what I could or couldn't do. No one knows what they will do until they're faced with a situation. You might say, "I'd never put up with my husband having an affair. I'd divorce him in a minute." It's easy to say what you would do IF—but you'll never really Know until it happens.

None of my reactions matched what I had expected. I did a much better job of coping with the initial information than I would ever have thought possible. I also had a growing rational understanding of the situation, but I remained tortured by my emotions. Even though I'd had an affair and could see how James did love me despite his affairs, it didn't erase the pain.

The memories continued to haunt me. I'd be doing just fine, and then something would happen to remind me of the past—and it would feel like it was happening all over again.

BEYOND AFFAIRS

The least little thing might trigger these memories. It could be a reference to a particular person or place or subject, or a color or a song—or a hundred other things. Invariably, it would bring back in full living color every detail of the painful feelings and events of the past.

This yo-yo up and down in my ability to cope with his affairs continued to keep me off balance for two or three years. There were times when things would be great and I'd think I was over the hump and had adjusted. Then...Bam! I'd get knocked all the way back down into a depression.

I frequently wished I could have amnesia. That seemed to be the only way I could forget the past. Also, I wished for time to pass. I'd always heard that time heals, but I never heard just how much time it takes. I didn't know whether I could last long enough. One of my fantasies was to suspend my life with James for about five years while I got over the past—and then pick it up again. This was impossible, of course, but it would have been my ideal solution to the dilemma I felt about continuing with our marriage.

While I could never quite bring myself to give up and get out of the marriage, it's clear I was willing to risk James getting so exasperated that he would decide to give up. Somehow I wanted the decision to be made for me—whichever decision it was. I simply couldn't decide on my own. Any real solution seemed impossible. I felt a need to completely erase the past. What I really wanted was for it "never to have happened." I was tired of trying to deal with it. Even divorce wouldn't bring an end to having to deal with it.

A divorce would just highlight the fact that it did happen and that it had affected my whole life. I would no longer be married and therefore would have a completely different life, but I would still have to deal with James (and the past) because of the kids. I had mixed emotions—feeling victimized by my memories and wanting to escape, but not wanting to give up after all the work I'd done. There seemed no way to resolve my dilemma. I felt trapped.

Please Truth Me

I finally got so desperate that I considered running away and taking a new identity—literally starting a new life. It seemed to be the only way to escape the tormenting reminders that were inevitable as long as James and I were together. I think one reason it got bad enough for me to consider this was because I hadn't done anything with my feelings. I'd talked about them, but that's different from acting on them—like screaming, or throwing things, or trying to hurt James in some way. I didn't want to do any of these things, but I felt a need to do something.

I came closest to taking action in the summer of 1975. We received a check for some joint consulting work. James was out of town. We had a second car—old, not in very good shape. I thought I really wouldn't be doing any harm if I took this old car and the check and started a new life.

Several things stopped me. One was the idea of losing contact with the kids. Another was my belief that things would eventually get better. The main reason for my hope was the consistent understanding and support James gave me during this struggle. He never said, "Shape up, it's been long enough now," or "How many times do we have to go through this?" or "I just can't keep talking about it; I've told you everything I can." He never said any of those things. If he had, I feel sure we wouldn't have made it. Instead, he kept loving me and talking to me and supporting me. He could see how hard I was trying—how well I had accepted everything intellectually, but how hard it was to deal with my emotions.

We spent many, many hours talking about our feelings and trying to get a handle on the whole experience. Little by little it got easier to handle the emotional aspects too. I don't know whether it will ever be completely dealt with. But I believe the process of writing this book has helped tremendously in putting it in perspective and making it more tangible and manageable.

Some people have asked why I even tried to work through it. They thought I should have gotten out. It's very

BEYOND AFFAIRS

clear to me why I stayed. When James told me about his affairs and came to understand the pain they had caused, he literally became a different person. He became all I could possibly want in a man. He was totally honest and fair with me, he loved me completely, and he was committed to doing everything in his power to support me in whatever I wanted in life. He wanted me to be happy, no matter what kind of life I chose.

I realized I might never find another man who would reach that degree of caring. I'd be foolish to give him up after he changed his way of relating to me. I could wish he's always been this way so I wouldn't have to accommodate to the two different people he represented in my mind. But that kind of thinking is as unrealistic as the "happy ever after" fairytales. No one gets everything they want in life, and this life with him gives me more of what I want than any other.

I'll probably always wish none of this had happened. The philosopher Nietzsche said: "That which does not kill me, makes me stronger." For the first three years I thought it might kill me—but it didn't. I'm a stronger person today for the experience, and our relationship is stronger too. That's not to say I would have chosen to have all this happen. But I'm reminded of a poster I once saw that said, "If life gives you a lemon, make lemonade." This experience was a bitter lemon, but some very good things have resulted from using it to make something better. Nothing is more refreshing than the kind of honesty we have now.

I've been asked, "How can you ever trust him again?" What I trust is his honesty—that he will never deceive me again. If he were promising specific things he would or wouldn't do, I couldn't trust that. Nobody knows absolutely what they will or will not ever do. But he's promised me honesty.

The real key to trusting this honesty is that he doesn't just say it—he practices it. He never hesitates to answer any question I ask him...about anything. He doesn't try to avoid issues that he thinks might upset me. He's willing to

Please Truth Me

"eyeball" me on any subject I want to discuss. The hours and hours he spent answering my questions about affairs earned him my trust in his honesty and helped me overcome my pain.

James:

I wrote the following piece on trust in August, 1973, during a flight from Pittsburgh to Hilton Head. It came out of my thinking about how we develop trust in general and my relationship with Peggy in particular. It had been germinating and influencing some of my actions for four or five years, but hadn't become strong enough to completely change my "double standard" ways. Six more months passed before I finally looked at the inconsistencies between my beliefs and actions. Since that night in January, 1974, when I acknowledged this to Peggy, I think I have lived the thoughts in Please Trust Me. So has Peggy...and it's made all the difference. Our trust is like a solid place to stand in a constantly shifting world.

Please Trust Me

Please trust me, so that I can love you freely. I need your trust to grow; without it I cannot be myself.

Your trust sets me free...gives me strength...helps me open myself to you... makes me rich...makes me feel ten feet tall...helps me accept myself...feels good I want to trust you. I will trust you if you care. I need clear expressions of your caring for me.

I will trust you if YOU share...l want to know who you are, what you feel, what you want, what you think...about life, about love, about me.

I will trust you if you dare... We will change and grow together if we are not afraid

I want you to be part of my becoming I want you to take the risk of hurting me in order to help me grow.

BEYOND AFFAIRS

I want to be part of your becoming. I will try to accept you as you are and help you become who you want to be. Please let me.

I will never hurt you on purpose, but I will run that risk in trying to help you grow.

I will make my trust known to you... with my eyes.., with my touch.. with my presence.., with my words.

My trust for you will endure over time and become stronger each time we renew it.

It needs to be renewed so that it will reflect the changes in each of us.

If I should lose your trust the weight of the loss would lie heavy on my shoulders.

Yet I would still be richer for having had it. I will not do anything knowingly that would cause you to lose trust in me. If I trust you deeply I will also love you deeply. Trust is a delicate thing.

I may say or do something sometimes that causes you to doubt my trust.

Please share that doubt with me and check out my intentions. I don't want to lose your trust.

There is no end to the depth of trust we can build Each time you show your trust in me my love for you grows deeper and I grow stronger.

Trusting you makes it possible for me to trust myself and others more.

When I trust my feelings and natural impulses and act on them, things usually turn out better. That's hard to do sometimes. Your trust helps me do it more often.

I need your trust now. Time will never permit us to Know each other completely.

But time need not stand in our way. I have trusted deeply after four hours of sharing. I have also found trust lacking after four years of working together.

I don't need to Know everything you have been or everything you might become. Let me Know you now, and I will trust you now.

Please Truth Me

I know we need some time together, and yet our ability to trust seems almost independent of time. Trusting feels good...not trusting feels awful.

Experiencing deep trust with you makes me feel like...time is standing still...we are touching something precious...we are reaching out for the highest part of being human...we are one with the universe.

I can feel your trust when you're not around...it feels like warm sunshine.

When you touch me gently you affirm your trust in me. I need your touch. I want it. It feels good.

There is power in trust-awesome power. I can do much, much more when I Know you trust me. I will stretch myself to keep your trust.

I want to be all the things that I cart. You can help me if you trust me. I hope you will.

As I learn more about myself, I will be able to trust you more. Please help me learn.

Peggy:

We were learning a lot about ourselves and each other as we pursued our commitment to honesty. We spent long hours talking through our feelings—not only about the past, but also about our future. One important factor in being able to devote this much time to these discussions was the complete change in lifestyle we developed after moving to Hilton Head.

Moving from Pittsburgh was like stepping off a merry-go-round. We avoided the cocktail-party circuit and concentrated on being together. And we drastically changed the way we related to our kids. Vicki was eleven and Andy was nine when we moved. In Pittsburgh, we had to work at integrating them into our lives. But on Hilton Head we literally took them everywhere we went and included them in everything we did. Instead of socializing with another couple, we socialized with them. Since our office was at home, they were part of our work life too.

BEYOND AFFAIRS

James:

We were concerned the kids might overhear us talking about the affairs or see something we were writing. We also thought they might sense the tension between us following some of our long discussions during that first year. We felt we should tell them about it as soon as possible, but it was a problem of timing. For about a year after I told Peggy, we weren't ready. There were too many unanswered questions and we were still having trouble talking freely without becoming emotional. We needed to be "together" enough to tell them without giving them the impression their world was falling apart.

Well-intentioned parents often try to protect children by withholding information from them indefinitely. The reality is, children are far more perceptive and aware than most adults realize. They are especially good at picking up cues we give out when we're trying to hide something. Our words say everything's OK, but our non-verbals say something's wrong. The anxiety children feel when they pick up these inconsistencies can be worse than their knowing the truth we're trying to protect them from.

Unfortunately, there are no absolute rules that define when a child is ready to deal with a certain kind of information. They need to have a way to relate it to the world as they are learning about it. Each child is unique and becomes ready according to an individual pattern of development. Probably the best way to judge readiness to deal with a new area is to watch for clues from them such as questions and comments related to the issue. It was easy to pick these up in this case. After being on the island for about two years, Andy and Vicki began to notice and comment on the number of their friends whose parents were divorced or separated. They paid particular attention to one friend's parents who were separated and dating openly. The island is like any small community in this regard. Everything one does with others is pretty visible to all.

Please Truth Me

After several comments and questions from them at different times, Peggy and I agreed they were ready...and so were we. We still wanted to deal with it in the most natural way possible, so we waited until they brought it up again. It happened in December of 1975. Andy was eleven and Vicki was thirteen. One of them made a comment at lunch about parents dating other people outside their marriage, so we proceeded to tell them we had done that too. It felt like a natural extension of the honest, adult communications we were developing with them. We were able to do it from a position of togetherness without the fear they would raise additional questions we weren't prepared to talk about.

Peggy:

They took it very casually—almost as if they hadn't really comprehended what we said. But they had understood, all right. Vicki told us later she'd had more difficulty in dealing with her Dad's affairs than she acknowledged when we told her. She hadn't wanted to say anything at the time because she could see how well I was handling it and she didn't want to make it more difficult. She needed time to think it through on her own. Andy's reaction was simply a "really...are you kiddin'?" kind of attitude.

We felt good about our decision to tell them. We wanted them to have a good understanding of life and love—not like the fairytale image we'd grown up with.

James:

I guess it's typical for parents to want their kids to have it better than they did. The big question is, "What's better?" We made three key decisions on their behalf. First, we decided that as much naturalness as possible about their bodies was a positive thing. So we began when they were babies to treat nudity as a natural state. We never made an issue of it. We simply went about the business of living. Where nudity was a natural part of our activity, they were never excluded—except when we were having sex. Even today, it would be unusual if one or both of our kids didn't come into our bedroom-bath area in the morning or at night while we're in the nude. It's our normal way of life.

Second, we wanted them to be well-informed about their own bodies and sex in general. We've tried to anticipate their need for information so they wouldn't have to pick it up at school and on the street. They have access to our books on male-female sexual functioning as well as some we bought specifically for them. We've put most emphasis on developing a climate where they can talk about any aspect of the topic that currently interests them. I give Peggy most of the credit for the success I think we've had in this area.

Third, we wanted them to know that sex doesn't end when you become a parent. This was as much for our sake as theirs. We didn't want to sneak around to have sex and we didn't want to deny our sexual sides in their presence. As soon as they were old enough to understand, we began locking our bedroom door and telling them whenever we wanted privacy for lovemaking. We haven't made a point of telling them the details of our sex life, but when it's been relevant to a question or issue they were dealing with, we've shared that too.

They still have difficulty thinking of us as sexual beings. I suppose they'll always see us as parents first. That's OK, but I hope close behind that image is another of a loving couple who express their love with enthusiasm.

Peggy:

It's a shame that many people assume sex diminishes in pleasure and importance with length of marriage and with age. Many young people grow up thinking this way and become adults who let it happen in their own lives. It's a self-fulfilling prophesy.

I know each generation—really each individual—must learn from their own experience. But we hope our honesty with our kids is allowing them to learn some things from our experience. For example, I've talked a lot with them about the importance of getting a sense of their own independence before committing themselves to another person. I've told them how much I regret not doing that myself—just expecting James to "make my world." They've watched me struggle with this issue as I've tried to get a clear sense of myself after all these years.

They should have a more realistic understanding of marriage than we had by virtue of all the sharing we've done with them. It's already made it easier for them to tell us about their thoughts and concerns. The communication we have with them as teenagers is one of the things I value most in life.

I recognize their right to engage in meaningful contact with the opposite sex. I don't want them to feel sneaky or guilty about their own sexuality. I want them to be loving, caring people who engage in relationships of their own choosing in the way of their choosing. Sex and loving can bring the most pleasure in life—or the most pain. I've seen both sides, and have a growing appreciation for the importance of giving this subject the attention it deserves.

James:

Having an honest, satisfying, male-female relationship in our society has been next to impossible. The stereotypes and prejudices we grow up with make it extremely difficult to ever see the other person as he or she really is. The games we learn to play make our interactions anything but honest. And the myths we've been taught about love relationships continually keep us from dealing with what's really happening. We deny the truth while hoping and dreaming for the impossible.

Peggy and I place a high priority on honest communication because of the tremendous impact it's had on our lives. Since I first opened up to her, we've completely redefined our relationship. Honest communication has been the primary process we've used and continue to use. It's led us to realize our relationship can never be a fixed thing—that it will always be in process as each of us continues to grow and change.

In traditional marriages, fixed roles give many people feelings of security and stability. The current divorce rate suggests that there's more illusion than reality to these feelings. It was frightening to give up the roles we had used to define ourselves for almost nineteen years of married life. At times we both felt it was simply asking too much. Our world seemed to be coming apart at the seams and we weren't sure we could put it back together again—or that we would like the new version better than the old. At the same time we knew in our hearts and guts that we were onto something significant. And it felt right. Rock-bottom, honest communication was like a totally new path opening up before us. It wasn't a very smooth path and we couldn't see very far ahead. We were tempted to leave it many times, but something kept us hanging in.

Gradually, honest communication and a commitment to equality have replaced fixed roles as the cornerstones of our changing relationship. We've had to give up some of our most cherished expectations in the process, but we've gained some things, too. We have a new kind of glue that holds our relationship together. We have a firmer base for acknowledging and supporting our individuality and our different needs to grow. Our commitment is to ourselves as individuals, to each other, and to our relationship—in that order.

I believe Peggy will support me in any direction I want to go in my life. I will do the same for her. I do not expect her to subvert her own values in supporting me and I do not expect our relationship to remain the same. Accepting that change is the way of the world and sharing a commitment to deal with our change openly and honestly has given us a greater sense of trust than we ever had with the fixed roles of our traditional marriage. Admitting out loud that there are no guarantees has stimulated us to create the most satisfying relationship we can, knowing that we'll never "arrive."

Peggy:

It took quite awhile for me to realize that one reason I had so much difficulty in escaping the past was that I was still caught up in my old roles to a great extent. My awareness of this was stimulated by the work I was doing with women in business. In 1975 I began writing a newsletter for women. I also wrote training exercises on assertiveness, career commitment, and support systems. With every new venture I recognized more of the aspects of my own life that were self-limiting and self-defeating.

James and I had each made some changes. But it became clear we needed to make a lot more. Old habits were hard to break. It was as hard for me to give up some of the "duties" with which I had identified as it was for James to take them on. As I began doing some independent traveling in my work, I was still trying to do almost everything I'd always done at home. It took a major event—my attending summer school at the University of South Carolina in Columbia in 1977—to change our pattern of living. With James and the kids together for the summer and me away at school, it cleared the way for a fresh start in defining our responsibilities.

James:

Morris Massey, in his excellent film, What You Are Is Where You Were When, defines a significant emotional event as a sort of mental arrest where we're forced to step back and look at the world from a different perspective. Peggy's affair had been such an event, and her summer in Columbia was another. Try as we might, we had been unable to break out of our old roles. The summer apart did the trick.

BEYOND AFFAIRS

Peggy:
We didn't try to "divide" household tasks by making lists. Instead, we did them together. We took joint responsibility for shopping, cooking, cleaning, yard work, and paying bills. We developed a simple system of making the bed together each morning so that it took about thirty seconds instead of two or three minutes for one of us to do it alone.

We involved the kids in our plan. We left the care of their clothes and their rooms completely up to them. This was more than just transferring housework. It was adopting a different attitude toward it. There was no hassling the kids to do these things our way or according to our standards. They had charge of when and how it would or would not get done. This gave them a sense of independence along with the responsibility. They thought it was a good deal.

These may seem like simple adjustments, but the total impact was significant. It diminished the amount of time and attention given to these tasks and gave all of us some new ways of relating.

My being away at school for that one summer made it easier to get these changes started. I continued my studying in the fall, but remained at home to do it. For the next two years I participated in the Adult Degree Completion Program of Antioch College, a non-residential program.

For many years I'd had mixed feelings about the prospect of going back to school. Some of my resistance was based on being somewhat "put off" by James' degrees and not wanting to compete or buy into his system of success. But as I grew stronger and more confident in my ability to succeed with or without a degree, I felt free to decide to get it. I had learned a lot on my own through the years. The program at Antioch recognized this independent learning. It also allowed me to be involved in designing and being responsible for my own course work. I completed the work for my B.A. in Psychology and attended the graduation ceremonies in 1979. It had been exactly twenty-five years since I graduated from high school.

James:

Peggy's work at Antioch was a natural extension of the self-study she had been engaged in for the past six years. As usual, she did it with gusto. Her development as a trainer and consultant has been a source of much pleasure and stimulation for me. We are professional colleagues in the truest sense. We're also "bookaholics" and enjoy sharing our reading. Since we both work out of an office in our home, we frequently go for fairly long periods when each of us is the only professional sounding board the other has. So far, this has worked well.

Being professional colleagues and working at home is not all positive, however. We're fighting pretty severe cases of "workaholism," and sometimes we're not so good for each other. The office is too convenient, and it's too easy to engage in shop talk, when we should be doing something more important-like having sex.

Peggy:

Despite our sex being better than ever, James hopes it may someday be possible for us to have sex with others. He thinks I'11 continue to put the past behind me and reach a point where I won't be so affected by what happened. I'm willing to admit anything is possible. But I can't imagine the hassle of trying to coordinate our lives with outside involvements. Also, I just don't have any big desire to have affairs. A desire I do have is for more privacy and alone time—a chance to function more independently.

James:

I'm very sympathetic with Peggy's desire to have some good blocks of time when she's really on her own. Getting married at nineteen kept us both from learning a lot about ourselves as independent people. At least I had the chance to finish school and develop my career. She rightly feels she gave some of the prime time of her life strictly in a support role. Of course, it won't be the same now, but I want her to have the freedom to do some things she wants to do.

At least once a month Peggy wishes out loud that we had a cabin in the woods where she could go and be alone—to write and think. I want her to have that time. Even if I have to be celibate while she's gone, I want it for her. She'll learn some important things about herself and life that will enrich both our lives when we're together. And that's the bottom line.

Peggy:
My experience of living alone the summer I went away to school was very positive. My living conditions were basic. I lived in a small apartment that was not air conditioned. I had no car. I rode my bike seven miles round trip to classes each day. I studied, ate, and slept. And I loved every minute of it—simply because I was on my own for the first time in my life. I'd like more of that kind of experience. So if the time comes when James feels strongly about having affairs, I'd probably choose for us not to live together.

That doesn't mean I'd want to end the relationship. I've thought carefully about that, and it's clear I want James to be part of my life all my life. But I would not want to be in the typical, live-in wife role trying to deal with lovers—either his or mine.

James:
The idea of not living with Peggy doesn't appeal to me. Not that I want to spend every day with her. I enjoy some time apart, as she does, but I get enough of that in the normal course of our travel. We're apart about ten days per month on the average, simply consulting and attending conferences. When I look at the days blocked off on the calendar, my gut reaction is—enough already. I want to

increase the quality of the time we have together, not decrease the quantity.

I understand that Peggy is an autonomous person and will seek to meet her own needs. I believe she will respect my needs in the process and will not consciously pursue hers at my expense. No one understands me or has my interests at heart more than she does. I trust her. I love her. I begin each day with a little more confidence and anticipation, knowing she's with me. If you have a spiritual connection like this, you know what I mean.

I don't pretend to know everything that went into the making of our bond. We've shared some big chunks of life together, including having and raising Vicki and Andy. I suppose everything we've done together has had some effect on it. I'm convinced that the most significant factor has been our commitment to honest, gut-level communication. That was the real beginning of the sense of oneness we have now. I know it sounds contradictory for me to describe how much I value my bond with Peggy and still say I want to have sex with other women. That's a good example of what comes from honest communication-seemingly crazy, contradictory, sometimes unrealistic expressions of thoughts and wishes. She understands that I'm not making demands on her or our relationship. I'm honestly stating what I want. I realize I can't have everything I want. If we never work it out, I'll live. But wanting sex with other women doesn't make me a bad person. It demonstrates I'm human—perhaps unrealistic, but not bad or immoral.

I think it might help you understand my position if you'll keep in mind that I always preface my statements to Peggy with these words: "If I could have everything I wanted.. " Even so, it's still a difficult subject to discuss calmly. I think I always scare myself more than her. And I know I feel more shaky than ever trying to put my thoughts in writing—to be read by people who don't know me the way she does.

I want to have sex with other women, but only under certain conditions—the main one being that it not interfere with the bond we have. The key is, our bond doesn't depend on sexual fidelity, and I believe it's strong enough to enable us to include other sexual partners without the gripping anxiety and fear society taught us to associate with sexual infidelity. I think we've reached that level of trust and commitment only recently. We thought we had deep trust in the early years of our marriage. It was really a surface trust, since we didn't know ourselves well enough to make the kind of commitment we have now. It was idealistic, based more on the notion of romantic love than shared values and goals.

Things were somewhat different when Peggy had her affair with Max. We had been communicating honestly for seven months, but hadn't yet reached some of the understandings we have today. I had thought we were ready, but I was wrong. It scared me half to death. In the years since then, we've had many hours of dialogue about our feelings and what would happen if we decided to have a sexually open marriage. I still think it's possible and I think we can do it.

But what I think is only half the story. Peggy also has to want it and believe we can do it before it would work. And right now, she doesn't. So for the foreseeable future, outside sex will remain only a possibility. The last thing I'd want is to pressure her to move in a direction she doesn't want to go. That would be a sure way to tear down or at least diminish the bond I want to preserve and build.

It's really a complicated issue. What I've discussed so far is only my primary condition—that we have outside sex only if we can do it without significantly diminishing our bond. There are other conditions that would be important to clarify, such as who, when, where, and how much. We would need to decide which people (only single people?), what times (only when we are separated by travel?), what places (only away from our home area?), and any other limits on degree of involvement and number of partners.

Please Truth Me

Peggy is right about there being some hassle involved. I don't think we could spell out all these conditions in advance. We would need to proceed with sensitivity for ourselves, each other, and the people we became involved with. The conditions would evolve as we had experiences and talked about them. I know I would still feel some fear and anxiety. We would need to support each other with continued demonstrations of our overall commitment. I think the anxiety would eventually diminish to very manageable proportions. It would probably never completely disappear. I'm not a pain freak, but I am a maximizer. I want to have the best relationship we can have and I'm willing to endure some discomfort in developing it. I've noticed that most change—even when it's positive—involves going through some discomfort before it feels natural and satisfying. I think the same is true here.

Very few people succeed in having sexually open marriages. Apparently the old jealousy monster is tough to subdue. That doesn't deter me. I. don't want to live my life just based on what others do or don't do. I want to live the life that's possible for me—and Peggy. I'm convinced that society's limits on sexual expression are artificial. They don't fit the human condition as I see it.

Sexuality is woven into the fabric of human interaction. To turn it on with Peggy and off with all other women is an arbitrary form of control. It doesn't allow me to follow my natural instincts in relating to others. Some of you are thinking, "Why does he think sex is so important?". The answer is—because it is. Not because I said so, but because it is. Look around you. The evidence is everywhere. Fulfilling sexual expression is a need present to some degree in all of us. When we're satisfying that need, we feel alive, connected and energized—ready to face the world. When we're not, we feel deadened, separate and depressed—sometimes wishing we weren't in the world. Some of you still ask, "Why can't we satisfy our sexual needs with one person?". Maybe you can. I'm not saying you ought to do anything other than what you choose. I'm expressing what feels right for me—what I want to try. I don't see anything unhealthy or morally wrong with having sex with more than one partner in an open, caring way. At least I want to try it, look at it as honestly as I can, and see for myself. With Peggy's agreement, I probably will. Without it, I won't.

Peggy:
James thinks we should be able to handle affairs. I think, idealistically, if you loved someone unselfishly, you'd be glad to have them do whatever made them happy. You wouldn't feel pride and jealousy and possessiveness. But I've been conditioned in this society, and just thinking I should be able to set aside my conditioning doesn't make it happen.

Another problem for me is the need I feel to protect myself from the kind of pain I've had in the past over James' affairs. I've dealt pretty well with the past, but I think it could come back to haunt me if I had to face dealing with affairs again. I know the honesty we now have would make a big difference. I wouldn't have the fear and insecurity I had during those other years. I even think if we were starting fresh now and I didn't have to worry about resurrecting the pain of the past—it might be OK. But we're not starting fresh. I still have some scars from the years when his pleasure was at my expense. I now have a strong commitment to looking out for myself, which means I only want good things for him if it's not at my expense. This doesn't meet the unselfish ideal I hold, but it's a reasonable result of things having been out of balance for so long.

My commitment to fairness, however, works both ways. While I don't want his pleasure to be at my expense, I'm also unwilling to get my way at his expense. By "get my way," I mean ruling out affairs indefinitely if he continues to want them. If he maintains this desire, at some point I would be unwilling to stand in his way. I don't want the responsibility for preventing him from having something he really wants in life. As it stands, he doesn't particularly want it now, but he

Please Truth Me

does want it at some point. Patience is one of his virtues. It's not one of mine. He is likely to be willing to continue in this undetermined state longer than I am. I don't like living with the knowledge that he is postponing something he wants because of me. I think it would eventually become a resentment he'd hold against me.

I try to avoid causing him to do other than what he chooses. Even in small things, I want him to do only what he wants. For instance, if I want to go to a movie that he doesn't particularly want to see, but he's willing to go along, then I specifically don't want him to go. It feels like a burden to have him accommodate to my wishes. I've seen how damaging too much "sacrifice" can be in a relationship, based on all the years I did it. I don't want that for anybody—even in something as critical as having affairs.

I continue to hope James will change and begin thinking more in the way I do about affairs. This is precisely the hope he has in the opposite direction—that I will change and begin thinking more like him. We don't know how this will eventually get resolved, but we have a lot of confidence in our ability to work on our differences in a constructive way. We'll continue to communicate openly and honestly about this and every other issue we face in the future.

We are committed to being a part of each other's lives from now on. This doesn't mean our relationship has to take some particular form—just that we won't cut ourselves off from each other. Working through the problems we've faced together has given us a sense of kinship that transcends everything else. It's brought a commitment that goes beyond our formal connection as husband and wife. I kiddingly suggested a way we could demonstrate that—by getting a divorce to celebrate our 25th Anniversary on May 29, 1980, and continuing to live together. That wasn't a practical idea because it would be misunderstood and create a lot of unnecessary complications. But it's a good feeling to know that we're together only because we want to be.

10

You're Not Alone

James:

We've gone well beyond the bounds of personal disclosure for most people in this book. We don't assume everyone should or will open up to the degree that we have. Our attitude toward disclosure is based on what openness has done for us. Opening up to each other has opened up the world. It's destroyed the illusion that we are alone and helped us discover the interconnectedness of everything. It's changed our way of looking at life by lowering and, in some cases, removing completely the boundaries we had accepted.

Each of us has a unique style of disclosing ourselves to others—letting them know us. It's a result of all we've learned from observing others and interacting with them. No doubt parents and family members had the strongest influence on us. My style determines what, how much, when, where, how, and who I disclose to. If our early disclosures are rejected or punished, we learn to withhold and hide our feelings and thoughts in an effort to play it safe.

If they are accepted and supported, we learn to reveal inner thoughts much more easily—without fear of rejection.

I believe most people have learned to constrain themselves too much—setting rigid boundaries that contribute to the feelings of isolation and aloneness that are so prevalent today. This keeps us from discovering what we have in common and inhibits our learning from and supporting one another. Call it anything you want—"playing it close to the vest," "being discreet," "being reserved"-disclosing at a low level is a limiting way to live. By holding back, we run the risk that others may never know us well enough to support our efforts to get what we want in life.

Now that I've acknowledged my bias for higher levels of disclosure, I also want to describe what I see as the risks and problems involved in it. The biggest problem for many of us is that the interpersonal skills we've learned are geared for relating in a low-disclosing way. Making the shift to a higher level of disclosure requires learning some new skills. Clear communication-especially about feelings—is a must. Many men have been conditioned to hide and deny their emotions so completely, they can't even understand what we mean by "talking through your feelings."

Disclosing at a higher level is not a panacea for improving all relationships. In fact, it's reasonable to expect that it will lead to the breakup of some. As we talk directly about our wants and values, we'll discover differences in some of our relationships that had been masked with low disclosure. If the relationship isn't important to us, we may dissolve it instead of putting forth the effort to work through these differences. But at least we have the choice.

A high-disclosing relationship is not for everyone. If you consider yourself a "private" person—and you're satisfied with what you're getting from your relationships—you may have no desire to change your personal style. Many people feel this way. Opting for higher disclosure is not a decision to be taken lightly. It goes beyond just having more conversations. It requires a commitment to honesty and a willingness to spend long hours in dialogue with your partner. It starts with honest disclosure of yourself, but you must also learn to really listen to your partner's reactions and disclosures. This kind of listening can't be faked. When I opened up to Peggy, I had no idea what I was getting into. I thought I was a good listener, but I had a lot to learn.

We come to a love relationship with a unique set of values, beliefs, needs, hopes, and fears. Because of the complexity of all these factors, it's impossible to disclose yourself completely, even if you wanted to and tried with all your might. What's needed is appropriate disclosure on a continuing basis on all the issues of importance in the relationship.

Here are some guidelines for honest communication in a high-disclosing relationship. They're not intended to be absolute or complete. They generally describe the way our communication has evolved.

1. Talk in great detail with your partner about your hopes and fears—what you want and don't want from the relationship. Invite the same in return. A high-disclosing relationship requires a mutual commitment. One partner can start it, but can't make it happen.
2. Expect resistance in yourself and your partner. We can never know for sure how another will react to our disclosures. It's normal to feel fear and anxiety when the stakes are high and we're reaching deep inside. Most of us have learned to avoid disclosure that may lead to discomfort. It seems safer at the time, but it's an illusion. Don't let your fear block you from saying what you need to say. Not talking about a potential problem won't make it go away. In fact, it may do just the opposite. It may cause it to grow.
3. Use prime time for your discussions. Prime time means you and your partner have good energy to put into the dialogue. You're not tired or sleepy or preoccupied with something else.

4. Choose a place where you're comfortable and free from distractions. It's difficult enough for most of us to talk from our hearts and guts without the inhibiting effects of physical discomfort and interruptions. Don't underestimate the importance of the right time and place. High-disclosure dialogue requires a lot of energy. Feeling tired, pressed for time, and generally uncomfortable is more likely to lead to arguments and misunderstandings than effective communication.
5. Talk frequently. Thoughts, emotions, hopes, and fears change rapidly. Every conversation doesn't have to be a long one, but it's important to keep your partner up to date on what you're thinking and feeling.
6. Express your feelings and emotions freely in words. It's the best way to insure clear, clean communications. Holding back or masking your feelings is only partial communication and is likely to cause misunderstanding. Don't use loaded words which will predictably generate defensiveness in your partner. You'll learn which words are loaded by simply paying attention and checking it out.
7. Listen to the feelings and words your partner is communicating. In some instances the feelings are more significant than the words. Look at your partner when he or she speaks or you'll miss a lot of the message. Touch when you feel the impulse. It's the ultimate way to communicate.
8. Accept full responsibility for your feelings and emotions. Don't blame your partner or expect him or her to take care of them. Don't try to "sugarcoat" a thought or feeling you think your partner will be negative about. It only prolongs the reaction.
9. Don't be afraid to say no when that's your gut response. Saying yes just to please someone or avoid some unpleasantness in the present can be disastrous when we know inside we'll eventually say no with our actions.

10. Ask your partner whatever you're curious about. Don't assume and don't guess. In the absence of knowing, we usually imagine the best or the worst—whichever suits our needs better at the moment. State the obvious. What seems obvious to you may not be so to your partner.
11. Support change in your partner. When you think your partner is taking a new position on something you've discussed before, by all means check for good clarity, but don't accuse him or her of being wishy-washy or of contradicting themselves. Change is natural and should be supported—not challenged.
12. Avoid absolutes in the form of demands or promises. They're tough to live by and they stimulate resistance and feelings of confinement. Absolutes are for saints, not fallible humans.
13. Don't expect your partner to read your mind. Ask for what you want or need, but don't be addicted to getting it. Give your own needs equal priority to those of your partner. Self-denial in relationships usually leads to resentment and moving apart. Self-fulfillment usually leads to greater love and capacity to give freely.
14. Don't sit in judgment of your partner. No one has that right. Judging and evaluating will surely decrease future disclosures and create defensiveness. You can and should express strong disagreement when that's your honest position, but you can do it without being judgmental.
15. Don't expect miracles. Gut-level communicating is hard work and takes time to develop in a relationship. It's likely to produce lots of anxiety in the early stages. There's a great temptation to back away at that point. The good news is—it gets easier. It eventually builds trust, predictability, and a tremendous problem-solving capacity in the relationship.
16. Expect some surprises. They're inevitable—no matter how much you think you know about your partner and

yourself. It may help to remember that while some will disturb you, others will delight you.
17. Don't forget to laugh. Relationships are serious business, but when we take ourselves too seriously, they can become too heavy to bear. Be prepared to play. A playful attitude is likely to be much more productive than a deadly serious one.
18. Be honest. This is the bottom line. Honesty simplifies life in the long run. Dishonesty complicates it. Being honest in a high-disclosing relationship means more than not lying. It means voluntarily talking directly about all issues of importance to the relationship.
19. Be generous with yourself and your partner. Don't be too critical if things aren't going as well as you'd like. Pause to savor every small success in breaking through the barriers. It will help you persevere when the going gets tough...and it will.
20. Start today. Don't wait on your partner to begin. Disclose something you've been thinking about, but holding back. It doesn't have to be startling. In fact, it's probably better if it's not. Increasing your disclosure a little each day will more likely lead to honest communication than trying to get there all at once. Don't insist that your partner agree to your goals of increasing disclosure. The chances are great that by taking the first step, you'll stimulate the same kind of response in return.

Differences that emerge between you and your partner will range across a broad continuum from insignificant to very important. Some will pose no problems. They're so slight, they don't matter—or their very existence adds spice to the relationship and enriches it. A lot of preferences fall on this end of the continuum. Your partner prefers a filet and you prefer a sirloin. I can assure you, you'll work that one out. Your partner prefers steak and you prefer fish. This will probably take some doing, but at least there's the possibility that you can both learn to eat something new and enjoy it.

You're Not Alone

Your partner prefers the Jersey shore for vacation and you prefer Florida. No big problem. Your partner prefers the shore and you prefer the mountains. Again, there's the possibility you can enrich your lives by learning from each other.

Life is not so simple at the other end of the continuum where we're dealing with deeply held values and preferences. Your partner prefers to live in the city. You prefer the country. It's where you grew up, what you understand, and where you feel alive. You're at home there, but the city drives you bananas. Even though you both want to work this out, now you're dealing with much more complexity and you may be amazed at how difficult it is to change some of these gut-level values. Sometimes we discover these differences early in the relationship and they are enough to keep us from continuing. Often we are well into the relationship before we face them squarely.

Raising children is a good example of a value-laden issue we can't really deal with until we have them—frequently several years after we're married. Agreeing to have children is simple compared to agreeing how to raise them. Many otherwise good relationships slowly disintegrate over the seemingly endless differences which arise, such as:

—When is the infant old enough to leave with a sitter?
—How much should you pay the sitter?
—How much should you spend on birthdays?
—How should you discipline a four-year-old?
—Should you spank?
—How much, if any, allowance should you give?
—How do you teach responsibility?
—How much work should a child do at home?
—How do you deal with problems at school?
—How do you discipline a teenager?
—How do you deal with use of drugs?
—How do you teach standards of behavior in such areas as personal cleanliness, sex, basic courtesy to others, etc.?

BEYOND AFFAIRS

—How do you set limits such as how many nights out per week, how late they can stay out, etc.?
—Should you force a teenager to attend church?

Many of the basic issues with children are ageless, but as the world changes, parents are continually confronted with new issues which no one anticipated. Reading books on raising children can help some, but you really have to be there before you know what you'll do in a particular situation.

In addition to the surprises that will come from sheer discovery, a couple committed to honest communication will find a lot to deal with based on the way each of them changes over the years. Here are a few examples:

—Both partners (in their early twenties) agree to delay having children for six or seven years—until they get established financially. After seven years of marriage, he wants to go ahead and have a child, but she's now involved in a career she doesn't want to interrupt...
—Another couple agrees to have three children. Two years after the first child is born, she is ready to have another, but he's decided one child is really enough...
—Another couple lives for twenty years in the traditional roles of breadwinner and homemaker. With their children away at school, she wants to take a job, but he resists. He can't accept the idea of his wife working...
—Another couple has worked hard for thirty years to achieve the good life. He's a vice-president of a large corporation. They live in the right neighborhood and belong to the right clubs. He decides he wants to chuck it all and move to the country. She can't understand what's gotten into him...

These kinds of changes can be difficult for any couple to cope with. Honest communication on a continuing basis can at least give each partner a chance to adjust to the other's change as it is occurring instead of being shocked one day with a grand pronouncement.

The big value issues can be tough to resolve, but they're not the whole story by any means. We're having more trouble with the nitty-gritty of living together every day. Take meals for example. We're both interested in nutrition, but Peggy is moving much faster than I am toward a completely different way of eating—lots of fresh fruits and uncooked vegetables whenever she's hungry instead of at regular mealtimes. I think it's the right direction, but I don't want to go that fast and I may not be willing to go as far as she does. We both like to eat out a lot, but I prefer restaurants with traditional fare while she prefers those that offer simple health foods. This should be enough to deal with around meals, but there's more. Money rears its ugly head. I'm comfortable paying the going rate for a good dinner at a fine restaurant. Peggy is not. She gets indigestion at the idea. Twenty years ago this issue didn't exist for us. I brought home the "bacon." Peggy cooked all the meals. We ate out as a treat once or twice a month and never gave a thought to nutrition. Now everything's up for grabs.

Assuming more responsibility for our health is another topic that has both of us excited. Use of time and money are two more that get our attention on a continuing basis. We agree in principle that we don't need a lot of money. We're intent on creating a simpler lifestyle that isn't encumbered with physical things. The question still remains, "How much is enough?".

Here's one other nitty-gritty many of you can relate to. For twenty years Peggy went along with my setting the thermostat. In the summer, I like it cool—OK, cold. She likes it hot. Now that she sees herself as a person of worth, she has the gall to ask why she should freeze in order for me to be comfortable. It's a good question. Needless to say, we're compromising.

BEYOND AFFAIRS

We've focused mostly on sex and affairs in this book. They're important topics, but for us they're only two among many ingredients that go into forming our quality of life. We're constantly rethinking all our values to see whether they're adding to or subtracting from our enjoyment of each day. This continues to be a clarifying, growing experience.

Peggy:
In reflecting on my efforts to get beyond the impact of James' affairs, I have a multitude of thoughts and feelings. First, I know I'11 never be the same—but that's not all bad. Much of it is good. Many people think finding out their partner is having an affair is the worst thing that can happen to them. That was not my experience. The isolation and rejection I felt when James first erected the barrier between us to protect himself from discovery was much worse. Without any clear suspicion that he was having an affair back in September of 1966, I had felt so desperate, I literally wanted to die. I didn't feel that kind of desperation when he finally told me in 1974. The difference was, I was a weak, insecure, anxious person in 1966. By 1974, I had gained a sense of my own worth.

I think the best survival tool for sustaining the trauma of your partner having an affair is to work on your own strength and self-esteem. If you see yourself as a complete person in your own right, you will not be destroyed by it if it happens. But if you see yourself only as an extension of your partner, then you're likely to feel your world is falling apart. You can't control another person, but you can take charge of yourself. Then you'll be able to handle whatever happens.

I found that coming to accept what had happened to me meant going through several stages, much like the stages of dying described by Elisabeth Kubler-Ross. Any death implies loss, and I had suffered the loss of my cherished illusions about marriage. First, there was denial and isolation. I didn't want to believe James was having affairs, and I kept my fears to myself. Then I felt anger and resentment that he would do such a thing. Then I began bargaining in my own mind, "If only he won't embarrass me until he can get over this, I'll wait it out." Then depression when I realized he wasn't going to "get over" it. He still wanted to continue having affairs. Finally, acceptance when I got a more thorough understanding of all that had happened and changed my way of looking at myself and my experience.

I'm aware of another similarity with the experience of a person facing death. Frequently, they accept their situation before others around them can accept it. I've reached an acceptance of what happened to me, but some people I've told can't seem to...and don't really want me to. They want me to act as they think they would. In essence, they see me acting "on their behalf" and want me to save them from their own fears about affairs.

These fears are not limited to women. Many men also can't imagine dealing with this situation in reverse. But increasing numbers of men will be faced with it as more and more married women become involved in affairs. Also, there are many couples who are not married but have a strong commitment to each other—and affairs are an issue for them too.

I'm aware of the problems that are common to all of us—women or men, married or single. Nevertheless, my comments are addressed to married women—because this is the base of my experience and the only one from which I can speak personally. I hope those who don't fit into that specific group will allow for my frame of reference—and include themselves in anything that fits for them. All of us who have dealt with affairs share a common need to prevent our experience from haunting us for the rest of our lives. We need to find a way to get rid of whatever pain and bitterness it caused. Knowing you're not alone and getting a better understanding of the factors involved in affairs doesn't do away with the pain they cause, but it does give you something to balance the pain so it doesn't overwhelm you.

I think there are two major keys to coping with affairs. First, you need to develop confidence in yourself as a separate person apart from your role in the relationship. You need to see yourself as strong, capable, and independent rather than weak, insecure, and dependent. You need to like yourself and feel able to cope with life in general.

Second, you need to strive to understand as much as possible about affairs in general and your own experience in particular. The first impulse may be to avoid knowing too much in an effort to avoid pain. But as long as you try to avoid it, it continues to have the power to disturb you. The more you learn about affairs, the more tangible and manageable they become. They're no longer a mysterious force eating at your insides, but real situations that you can put in perspective.

You may have a natural tendency to hide the fact that your husband has had an affair (or that you think he's having an affair). It's a terrible blow to your pride. It feels like something you should be ashamed of. You feel rejected, unloved...and unlovable. You may think, as I did, "Why me? How could he do this?" or "Where did I go wrong? Where did I fail as a wife?" I found that I had to talk through these feelings in order to get beyond my pain and confusion.

Sometimes this can be done with your husband, as I did. At other times, that would be absolutely impossible. He might not be willing, you might not be willing, or you might not feel capable of working through it together. You may feel uncomfortable in talking to a friend, a minister, or even a counselor about it—because it strikes at the very core of your feelings of worth as a person. You may assume that no one else can understand your pain—that no one else has felt the anger, the resentment, the bitterness, the unfairness of it all. You may feel terribly alone.

But you're not alone! There are thousands of women who share this common experience...and there are many counselors who have dealt with this issue. We can seek help from understanding professionals who are sensitive to our feelings, and we certainly can share with each other in a way that isn't possible with someone who hasn't "been there." Sharing with other women who have had similar experiences can have a strong healing effect. This kind of sharing can take place with one woman or a group of women—with friends or with strangers. The important thing is to come together to support each other in working through your feelings.

Men whose wives have had affairs frequently have similar feelings to deal with. The conditioning men have received to act strong and deny their need for help makes it difficult for them to get the support they need. The damage to their pride may feel too devastating. But the sense of isolation in dealing with it alone may keep them bogged down for years. They can benefit from sharing in a group with other men, just as women can with other women.

The power in a group is that you see other people at different stages of recovery. You'll see some who are like you—some who are better off—and some that are a lot worse. You can get a perspective that isn't possible when dealing with it alone. And more importantly, you can get the support you need to get on top of your life and feel like a whole person again.

Here are some guidelines that might be helpful in such a group:

1. Be honest in your sharing. Avoid any tendency to "put up a good front." Don't compete by trying to sound better or worse off than someone else. Remember...you're all in this together and you don't have to impress anybody.
2. Support each other in feeling good about yourselves and your ability to cope with the situation. Self-confidence is vital in getting beyond the pain. This means not getting bogged down in "blaming" and griping about "how

awful it is." Acknowledging these feelings may be necessary and useful, but going over and over them doesn't change anything—and may do you harm. It can keep you feeling sorry for yourself, and this just makes it harder to develop your sense of self-worth.
3. Really listen to the other people in your group. You've come together to support each other. That can't happen if you're only thinking about yourself.
4. Don't debate differences of opinion. Being supportive means avoiding "approving" or "disapproving." There's no need to be in agreement. Support comes from understanding and accepting—not from judging.
5. Avoid "leading" questions or "helpful" advice, such as:
"Why don't you...?"
"Did you try...?"
"I think you should..."
"If it were me, I'd..."
6. Ask clarifying questions to help each person think things through for themselves, such as:
"How long have you felt this way?"
"Have you discussed this with anyone else?"
"What have you tried?"
"What are your alternatives?"
7. Talk about your feelings. That's more important than the details of your experience.
8. If you feel angry—admit it. You can't overcome it as long as you hide or deny it. This doesn't mean you have to act on it. Just openly acknowledging your anger is the first step toward loosening its power.
9. If you feel guilty—say so. You may be holding secret fears that somehow it's all your fault. Again, you need to acknowledge the feelings before you can deal with them. There are many burdens of guilt you may have put on yourself that you need to get rid of. You could feel:
—guilty that you failed to have the "ideal" relationship.
—guilty that you're leaving your partner.
—guilty that you're not leaving your partner.

—guilty that you feel angry or vindictive.
10. Freely respond to others when they express feelings that you understand or can identify with. This may not seem very important, but it can be critical in giving them the strength they need and letting them see they're not alone. You can offer comments, such as:
"I know how you feel."
"I've had that experience too."
"That's one of my concerns...or fears...or uncertainties."
11. Remember that the group cannot decide how you should feel or what you should do. It can provide support for you to figure things out for yourself.

James and Peggy:
What can we say in summing up?
—That if you confess your affairs, you and your love partner will live happily ever after No! Replacing one myth with another doesn't help anything.
—That if you're completely honest, everything will work out? No! Total honesty can be terribly destructive and should never be practiced indiscriminately.
—That if you have an affair and then work through it with your partner, it will improve your relationship No! Having affairs, whether or not you talk about it, is just as likely to destroy the relationship as to improve it.
—That if you have a good relationship, you'll never have to worry about affairs No! There are no guarantees.

Getting BEYOND AFFAIRS doesn't mean getting beyond the possibility of ever having it happen to you. It doesn't mean just getting beyond the immediate decision of what to do about it. It means getting beyond the power it can have to affect you in a negative way—with anger, bitterness, hurt, or shame—for the rest of your life.

BEYOND AFFAIRS

You can get beyond all that. You can be a strong, confident person who has a good grasp of what happened to you and how your experience was affected by the attitudes and norms of our society in general. Affairs are not as "personal" as we have made them by our secrecy. If you've "been there," you're part of one of the largest groups of people in this country. In this sense, you're not alone.

In another sense, you are alone. In the final analysis, dealing with affairs is a very individual, personal thing. No matter what support or "advice" you get from others, it's still up to you to make your own decisions. There are many people who will tell you what you "ought" to do—especially if they haven't had to deal with it themselves. Also, there are plenty of people who have dealt with it and think they know THE answer. We are under no such illusion. Our effort has not been to tell you what you should do. We have tried to present some alternatives to the obvious choices of "swallowing your pride and ignoring it" or "getting a divorce." Whatever decision you make about your actions, our hope is that it will allow you to put the experience behind you and get on with your life.

Epilogue:
Update 30 Years Later

Up to this point, everything in this book is the same as the original publication in 1980. At that point we had been married 25 years. Now, 30 years later and married for 55 years, we recognize the need for an update. So we have added this Epilogue to tell 'the rest of the story.'

The most prevalent personal question I've been asked since the original publication is: *"What has your marriage been like since you dealt with the affairs? I wonder whether you have been monogamous all these years?"*

The answer is Yes. We've had a monogamous marriage during all the years since the affairs ended in 1974. At that time, James and I made a different kind of commitment, not to "monogamy," but to "honesty."

Here's the way I described this commitment in *The Monogamy Myth*:

BEYOND AFFAIRS

"Honesty was the motivator for my husband telling me about his affairs. We also relied on honesty as a way of working through all the feelings that had built up through the years. And honesty was the basis of our commitment to the kind of relationship we wanted to develop in the future. While I wanted a monogamous relationship, I recognized the fallacy of a promise of monogamy. So James didn't promise to be monogamous; he promised to be honest. But the result of our commitment to honesty has led to our being monogamous during the years since that commitment was made.

"The way to rebuild trust is not by making a promise of monogamy, but by making a commitment to honesty. There's a tendency to think of honesty only as telling something that was previously kept secret. But the main power of honesty is in sharing feelings. When a couple share their deepest feelings about everything, including the "scary" stuff (like attractions to other people or fears of their partner having an affair), they develop a deeper understanding of each other.

"Many people think that talking about such emotional issues will inevitably cause problems. But it's far more likely that it will lead to a closer relationship because of the comfort involved in feeling you will be told the truth about anything that comes up. Honesty is much more than simply not lying; it's not withholding information or feelings that are important to the relationship.

"Our honesty is not restricted to issues related to affairs; we're honest about everything relevant to our relationship. This includes talking about our personal hopes and dreams as well as our private fears and anxieties. While this kind of honesty brings a special bond to a relationship, there's a personal benefit as well that is often overlooked. Honesty provides a firm place to stand

Epilogue

in the world. It forms a solid basis from which to embark upon the challenges of everyday life.

Going Public

With the initial publication of this book in 1980, we began our commitment to using our experience to help others facing this issue in their own marriages. This involved our 'going public' in a significant way.

This public discussion began with an appearance on the "Donahue Show." In fact, when we appeared on "Donahue," James and I were the first couple to appear on a daytime talk show discussing their personal experience in dealing with extramarital affairs and staying together as a couple.

("Donahue" was the only daytime talk show on the air in those days. Almost everything about that 1980 show was different from today's talk shows. It was handled very responsibly, and we were the only two guests for the entire hour.)

The overwhelming reaction to our going public was quite unexpected. It seems that this degree of candor about affairs captured the fascination of a lot of people, including the public, the media, and the publishing world.

We had initially self-published *Beyond Affairs,* but after going public with our story, we were contacted by Bantam Books who wanted to publish it in paperback—which they did the following year, in 1981.

They sent us on a three-week national media tour, which led to making about a hundred other media appearances during the next few years. This allowed us to reach a large number of people, many of whom were eager to share their experiences with us.

In learning so much from the people who contacted me, I recognized the need for a book that went beyond my own experience. So in 1989, I wrote *The Monogamy Myth* in an effort to provide more perspective on the whole issue of affairs.

Since that time I have written many books and articles on affairs, including my latest book on preventing affairs, *To Have and To Hold*. I also founded an international support group, BAN (Beyond Affairs Network), and established an Extramarital Affairs Resource Center on DearPeggy.com, the website I launched in 1996.

Building a Stronger Marriage

Of course, it was not just my work life that changed. The experience of going public had an impact on our personal life as well. Our joint commitment to working together to help others led our bond to grow even stronger.

Some people might think that the ongoing focus on affairs (and reviewing our own personal experience) might be tough on our marriage, but just the opposite was true. All our work has brought us closer together and allowed us to build a stronger marriage than we had before.

It's always a little dangerous to suggest that a marriage can actually become stronger after an affair—because some people will use this as a way of "justifying" an affair, saying that it "helped" the marriage. I have never seen an affair "help" a marriage. What sometimes happens (as happened with us) is that the work we did together—and the rock-bottom commitment to honesty that we made together—did forge a stronger bond than we had had before. But it wasn't the affairs that helped our marriage; it was the way we dealt with this crisis that made it possible for us to grow stronger as a couple.

When someone is in the early stages of dealing with the devastating emotional impact of a partner's affair, it's difficult to hear that it's possible (with lots of time and effort by both people) to eventually come through this with a stronger marriage. On the other hand, it can be helpful to understand that it's possible for this to happen.

Epilogue

We want to be clear that we do *not* think we're "special" or "unique" in being able to rebuild a stronger marriage. A crisis like this can either destroy your relationship—or it can lead to actions that wind up strengthening it.

In fact, often it's not the crisis itself that has as much lasting impact on our lives as it is the way we *deal* with the crisis. So in the midst of the struggle to deal with current issues around an affair, it might help to think in terms of finding a way to eventually gain some *benefits* from the process.

Any crisis can be a wake-up call—a jolting moment that can become an opportunity for positive change. These moments don't feel like "opportunities" when you're in the midst of dealing with them. But it's a little like looking back when you're driving up a long, slow incline on the highway. You don't realize how far you've come until you look back at where you've been.

This realization can sometimes be helpful when you're still "climbing," but a crisis does have a way of putting things in a new perspective. It shakes up our world and leads us to rethink everything about our lives. The impact of an affair involves more than just dealing with the affair itself (as if that weren't enough); it's dealing with a whole new way of seeing yourself, your spouse, yourselves as a couple—even your place in the world.

Our lives today are the result of the depth of honesty in our relationship since those difficult years of dealing with the affairs. We maintain a special closeness through fully sharing with each other and feeling we truly know each other at a deep level.

I don't want this to sound like some kind of fairy-tale existence. It's not. *Everyone* has problems—and we've had our share. I've had breast cancer and James has had prostate cancer. In 2003 our son was having a heart attack, and had to have an emergency angioplasty to insert a stent, and two days later our daughter's house burned down in the Southern California wild fires.

However, we recognize that crises come to everyone, and we must all do our best to deal with whatever crises we face. All in all... my life and my marriage are good—but certainly it's not the life I would ever have envisioned for myself.

In fact, an early reviewer of *The Monogamy Myth*, who gave the book a very positive review, made a personal comment that pretty much sums it up:

"When some women's husbands have affairs, they get a divorce. Others stay married, but suffer in silence. Peggy Vaughan's husband had affairs—and she made a career out of it!"

Maintaining a Vital Sex Life

Dealing with the crisis of affairs led to a commitment to honesty that was aimed at rebuilding trust, but this commitment also applied to every aspect of our lives. An unintended consequence was that it enabled us to develop a special closeness and willingness to be vulnerable that enhanced the overall freedom and comfort of our sexual relationship.

This closeness is particularly valuable when you are forced to deal with the various issues that arise that can affect your sex life—like health problems and aging. So I'll discuss some of these issues and share our efforts to deal with them.

Breast Cancer:

In 1992, at the age of 56, I was diagnosed with breast cancer, and had a lumpectomy, chemo and radiation. During the 6-month period of treatment, our sex life continued as before. In fact, there was a certain "sweetness" associated with enjoying sex with a body that was in other ways struggling through the treatments. And my bald head resulting from the chemo gave me a kind of sweet, innocent appearance that made James even more caring and

Epilogue

protective of me, helping to increase our bond during this difficult time.

However, I must admit I felt a little awkward about the appearance of the breast that underwent surgery due to the fact that the surgeon acknowledged that he failed to do the kind of job (aesthetically) that he should have done. Of course, I appreciate that the overwhelming priority is the cancer itself, not the aesthetic results of the surgery. So while it was disappointing that the surgery left a crease across the center of the breast (which was a constant reminder of the cancer), I tried not to let it interfere with my sexual feelings.

This effort was greatly enhanced by the way James reacted to me during this time. He made it clear that he continued to find me attractive and sexually desirable. He continued to touch me in the same ways as always, and it was especially comforting to have those casual touches that had no overt sexual overtones. In fact, the non-sexual closeness we have always shared (with our morning ritual of cuddling when we first wake up) has no doubt been a factor in maintaining the kind of physical bond that also helps keep sex alive.

Another byproduct of the breast cancer was that the chemo plunged me into sudden menopause. Prior to that time, I still had regular periods and regular hormone levels, including those associated with stimulating sexual desire. In addition to a significantly reduced libido, I also experienced other common menopause-related symptoms like hot flashes, etc., that can undermine a woman's sense of herself sexually.

Unfortunately, many people assume that menopause means a certain decline in sexual activity. However, it only means you may not have the same *desire* for sex; there can still be *arousal*. And since a part of the capacity for arousal lies between your ears, not just between your legs, you can still have a very satisfying sex life. So despite not having the same impetus to embark on the experience, I learned to appreciate the results of going ahead anyway—thus our sex life did not suffer.

Prostate Cancer:

Another potential challenge came two years later when James was diagnosed with prostate cancer. None of the possible treatments are without some risks, many of them related to possible impotence. As with my breast cancer, the priority was to take care of the cancer, but the possibility of forgoing the kind of sex life you had previously enjoyed is an extremely serious issue.

Doctors don't "order" which kind of treatment to choose—either for breast cancer or prostate cancer. They may recommend one over the other—but frankly, the recommendations are often based more on their personal specialty than any other criteria. We did a lot of reading/studying/interviewing doctors and concluded that (even with the risks of impotence and/or incontinence) the best choice at his age and stage of life was a radical prostatectomy, the surgical removal of the prostate.

We were fortunate in that he had an excellent surgeon who was able to perform the surgery while leaving the all-important nerves intact, hopefully avoiding either of the common serious side-effects of this surgery. But, of course, we couldn't be sure about the potency until some time had passed—because it does take time (and attention) to restore full sexual functioning.

Unfortunately, most doctors adopt a kind of "don't ask, don't tell" policy when it comes to a man's sex life following surgery. This is simply not a topic the doctor normally addresses—beyond the initial information that the surgery has these possible negative side-effects. So following surgery, there was no discussion with the doctor about how things stood in the sexual arena.

We were fortunate in that our ability to honestly discuss the situation in the months following the surgery made all the difference in its impact on our sex life. Having already

Epilogue

established an ability to candidly talk about our sex life put us at a significant advantage, quite different from some other men with whom we spoke about their experience following the surgery.

We knew from our reading that it might take some time to know the full impact on potency. So during the first months when erectile function was not sufficient for intercourse, we stuck to oral sex and other forms of sexual satisfaction. This was the nature of our sex lives for about nine months, at which time full erections allowed us to once again include intercourse.

Without the ability to talk through all aspects of this situation and continue a sexual relationship (with all the ongoing stimulation that provided), it's unlikely that intercourse would ever have been resumed. That would have been an unnecessary loss, one not usually discussed, which is one of the reasons for sharing this experience.

Weight and Fitness:

We are extremely fortunate that at this point (age 74) we both are healthy, fit and physically active. Even without facing a particular physical problem like side effects from cancer or other illness, every couple's sex life is affected by the physical condition of their bodies. Other than our bouts with cancer, James and I have been fortunate in maintaining our bodies in a way that is healthy and fit. A big part of our motivation for this was not for the sake of sex, but of life itself. I watched my mother gain about 150 pounds through the years, leading to diabetes, including blindness, and eventual death with gangrene. At that point she was 71 years old and weighed 270 pounds. And James's father, who was overweight as well, died of a massive heart attack at age 47. I'm sure our awareness of the health results for our parents played a major role in our ongoing efforts to maintain healthy bodies, which had the effect of also allowing us to function better sexually.

BEYOND AFFAIRS

Unfortunately, even the most responsible people sometimes fail to take care of their bodies. While people of all shapes and sizes certainly have and enjoy sexual relationships, the growing epidemic of obesity may lead many people to be so uncomfortable with their bodies that it negatively affects both their partners and themselves in their openness to and enjoyment of sex. In fact, those who are extremely overweight may find the act of intercourse itself to be a physical challenge, further inhibiting their sex lives.

Effects of Aging:
The condition of our bodies plays an even greater role in our sex lives as we age. About the time we reached 60 (when many people accept the idea of a possibly decreased sex life), we determined that we were not going to sit idly by and allow that to happen. So we developed a plan—which continues today in our 70s. If we have sex sometime during any given week, fine. But if it doesn't happen spontaneously, we still have sex—because we have agreed upon a certain day of the week when it will happen.

This kind of plan to *choose* to have sex works well. In fact, it has some advantages in that (like dating) you know it's coming up and you anticipate it. For women especially, thinking about it in advance can help "get in the mood."

There have been rare occasions where something happened to interfere with our "sex date," but we've found that it only serves to make a spontaneous sexual experience more likely during the following week. And at the very least, having this kind of plan assures that we never let sex recede from awareness or attention—as happens all too often when couples just ignore the absence of sex in their lives.

Love and Sex:
Sex is only one of the ways couples show their love through the years. So none of these efforts may be effective unless you are simultaneously keeping *love* alive—not just

Epilogue

keeping *sex* alive. We talk a lot more about this in our book, *Making Love Stay*.

Our Lives Today

The kind of honesty we enjoy may seem scary to those who haven't considered it, but the payoff is enormous. It allows you to feel known and understood for who you really are. In fact, it actually provides a safe environment in which to enjoy all the other aspects of your life.

Let me make it clear, however, that the closeness we share in our marriage does not prevent our being individuals as well. In fact, too much *togetherness* can become "too much of good thing." Since we both enjoy alone-time, we try to arrange our activities to allow each of us to enjoy some independent activities and some quiet time as well.

Generally, we live simply, preferring to avoid the kind of business travel and public appearances we've done for so many years.

Most important, we're surrounded by our immediate family. We moved to Southern California in 1985 - so at this point we've been here 25 years. Our daughter married and moved here with her husband in 1986. And our son moved here in 1996.

We also have three wonderful granddaughters, and are so thankful to be grandparents who can enjoy the children *together*. If the affairs had led us to divorce, we would have missed out on so much of the richness of an intact extended family. So I feel particularly thankful that we were able to rebuild our marriage.

Our Future

At this stage of our lives, we feel extremely fortunate that we are growing old together. Actually, we don't *feel* old, despite the fact that we both just celebrated our 74th birthdays. I believe a big part of our well-being (both physically and mentally) can be attributed to having reached this point in our lives with the sure knowledge that we can handle anything!

I do believe that having faced and dealt with affairs, as well as both of us facing and dealing with cancer and other life issues, has given us confidence in our ability to deal with whatever else we may face in our lives.

I agree with the quote from Nietzsche: *"What does not kill me, makes me stronger,"* as well as a similar one from Ernest Hemingway: *"The world breaks everyone, and afterward, some are strong at the broken places."*

We definitely feel we are stronger, both as individuals and as a couple—and we look forward to our future together.

Grow old along with me! The best is yet to be, the last of life, for which the first was made.
—Robert Browning

Made in the USA
Lexington, KY
12 September 2010